KEEP ANY
PROMISE

KEEP ANY PROMISE

A blueprint for
designing your future

Karim H. Ismail

iUniverse, Inc.
New York Bloomington Shanghai

Keep ANY Promise
A blueprint for designing your future

iUniverse books may be ordered through booksellers or by contacting:

iUniverse
1663 Liberty Drive
Bloomington, IN 47403
www.iuniverse.com
1-800-Authors (1-800-288-4677)

Because of the dynamic nature of the Internet, any Web addresses or links contained in this book may have changed since publication and may no longer be valid.

The views expressed in this work are solely those of the author and do not necessarily reflect the views of the publisher, and the publisher hereby disclaims any responsibility for them.

ISBN: 978-0-595-46705-1 (pbk)
ISBN: 978-0-595-71947-1 (cloth)
ISBN: 978-0-595-91001-4 (ebk)

Printed in the United States of America

To:

My best friend, soul mate, spouse, and lover, Narmin,
wonderful mother to our two children, Aliya and Amaan;

My beloved aunt Nargis, whose encouragement, support, faith,
and belief in me have sustained me since my childhood;

My uncle Alli, whose support and overwhelming generosity gave me
a much-needed start in my then newly-adopted country, Canada.

"Our deepest fear is not that we are inadequate.
Our deepest fear is that we are powerful beyond measure.
It is our light, not our darkness, that frightens us most.

We ask ourselves, 'Who am I to be brilliant, gorgeous,
talented, and famous?' Actually, who are you not to be?

You are a child of God. Your playing small does not serve
the world. There is nothing enlightened about shrinking
so that people won't feel insecure around you. We are all
meant to shine, as children do. We were born to make
manifest the glory of God that is within us. It's not just
in some of us; it's in everyone.

And as we let our own light shine, we unconsciously
give other people permission to do the same.
As we are liberated from our own fear,
our presence automatically liberates others."

Contents

Part 2: How Do I Implement My Goals and Stay Focused?   87

Acknowledgments

I owe a huge debt of gratitude to Gail Nielsen, executive coach extraordinaire. Her story appears in Chapter 12. She is the catalyst for bringing this book to fruition, and her feedback through various drafts was invaluable. Thanks for putting my feet to the fire, time and time again, Gail.

I am particularly indebted to the twelve wonderful people from around the world who agreed to share their personal stories. I hope you will learn as much from their stories as I have. Their names appear below in the order of appearance in the book.

Audrey Loeb	Aziz M. Bhaloo	Murray Dryden
Bilaal Rajan	Nilofer Juma	Lisa Rowles
Frank Tielve	Maria Castella	Donna Duggan
Alli Amlani	Keith Rieger	Gail Nielsen

I received invaluable feedback on the book drafts from many people, which helped strengthen the book and worksheets considerably. My special thanks to:

Amee Sandhu, Toronto, ON	Lily Jain, Toronto, ON
Akbar Moosabhoy, Toronto, ON	Lynn Sanders, Chicago, IL
Arzina Murji, Toronto, ON	Mustafa Karim, Dallas, TX
Christie Scott, Houma, LA	Narmin K. Ismail, Toronto, ON
Elisa Palombi, Toronto, ON	Nimet Maherali, London, UK
Galib Rayani, Markham, ON	Shelina Kassum, Toronto, ON
Joanne King, Nelson, BC	Stephen Brown, Toronto, ON
Keith Rieger, Surprise, AZ	Tasneem Moosabhoy, Toronto, ON
Linda Robinson, Toronto, ON	Teri Katzenberger, Sioux Falls, SD

To Shaam Rodrigo at Eighty20, thank you for the cover design concept and book layouts. Your design skills made the book come alive. And to Zafar Abid, thank you for your help with the book Web site, www.KeepAnyPromise.com.

To the team at iUniverse.com, thank you. Your wisdom, feedback, and support are greatly appreciated. And to Bob Ramsay and Carol Ross, thank you for your help with editing.

Finally, to my daughter Aliya K. Ismail, my deepest gratitude for your encouragement, suggestions, edits, and multiple proofreads along the way. You have been a vital part of this journey.

Introduction

In 2002, only six years ago, I could not walk to the end of my driveway. I took huge and increasingly ineffective doses of morphine, which pumped through my body attempting to control my debilitating back pain. It began about twenty-five years prior. I was an active squash and badminton player. I played hard and I gave it my all. My back problems worsened, yet I kept pushing, playing hard.

I continued being active and enduring agonizing pain. Eventually, I ended up with severely damaged spinal discs. Flat on my back for months and being forced to stop any physical activity, I gained forty pounds. My family business was bleeding following the Internet crash of 2001. Business from our technology clients was drying up, and we were no longer able to commercialize new investments in technology. I was in pain and overweight, and my family's financial security was looking increasingly bleak.

While years of dedication and extreme hard work in my career and volunteer responsibilities brought me rapid promotions, titles, and much professional success at a young age, this success came at a price. My relationship with my childhood sweetheart, Narmin, was strained, and my children, Aliya and Amaan, were growing ever-distant from me. The deep spiritual connection I had developed as a child (a gift from my wonderful parents) had all but completely eroded. I was spiritually empty. I berated myself for my situation.

All my dreams and promises to myself lay in tatters. I felt increasingly unable to support my family and to afford the best possible university education for my children—a long-cherished desire. My dream of making a meaningful impact on the world was crumbling around me. I began thinking about the large supply of narcotics I had on hand to control my back pain. I thought frequently about how easy it would be to end my life—if only I had the courage to do so.

So … what are *your* unkept promises? Do you believe that you are making a substantial difference in the world, or have you long given up even trying? Do you spend most of your time doing the things you absolutely love to do, or are you stuck living life according to someone else's agenda? Do you pay regular, consistent attention to the people who matter most to you, or are you constantly neglecting your loved ones? Above all … are you keeping the promises that you have made to yourself throughout your life?

Recently, I asked myself these very questions. Despite having achieved much in the eyes of others, I felt confused. I was also very unhappy, completely unfulfilled, and extremely depressed.

One day, as I went for a short walk on a bitterly cold February morning, a thought struck me. Why was I so successful in my professional life but failing in my personal life? What was the magic formula I was using brilliantly in one realm but neglecting in the other? On my return, I got out my notebook and sat down to list the intuitive principles that had made me professionally successful. I counted the successes I had enjoyed over a twenty-year period, envisioning and overseeing the design and construction of healthcare and cultural buildings worth $750 million. I noted that many of these projects were architectural masterpieces by the world's best designers. Even in my despair, I realized that I already had a blueprint for success, one I had used every day for twenty years. Quite simply, I could develop a compelling vision, set clear goals, implement highly organized systems, and hold regular reviews. I had a knack for creating something from nothing.

I wondered: could I modify and apply these principles to my personal life so that I could begin to crawl my way out of these feelings of utter helplessness? Could I ever get back on track to fulfilling the big promises I had made to myself?

Gradually, I set about undertaking a major personal transformation. I started reading self-help and spirituality-oriented books. I attended self-development workshops, many of which provided life-altering thinking. Tony Robbins' *Unleash the Power Within* seminar was an emotional turning point for change. From my learnings and the professional skills I had developed, I was able to transform my blueprint for professional success into one for *personal* success. The journey was long, it was difficult, and it was painful, for it forced me to completely rethink who I was, what my priorities were, and my life purpose. The end result was a complete life transformation.

Today, I am an accomplished mountain hiker, having hiked Kilimanjaro and trekked in the Andes. I am almost pain-free and near my ideal weight. I have rediscovered my lost spirituality and I pray, meditate, and enjoy nature every day. I feel increasingly connected to a universal source. I have the closest, deepest family relationships I have ever enjoyed. Our family business serves a meaningful social purpose through our work with North America's finest independent schools. And we are close to long-term financial stability. Our children have graduated from some of America's finest universities and are launching promising careers. I hold strategic volunteer roles that I once again enjoy tremendously. I can again dream of making a huge world impact. In short, I am high on life, and I wish every day would never end!

During the last five years, as I shared my personal transformation with others, it quickly became apparent to me that I could use this blueprint to help others keep their promises. They would not have to live a life of broken promises, as I once seemed destined to do. So I set a huge goal for myself: I promised myself that within twenty years, I would help five million people transform their own lives using the skills I had sharpened while managing complex projects, the personal lessons I had learned, and the wisdom from experts that the universe placed in my path. I had no idea how I would keep this promise! But I knew this goal would be a huge part of helping me fulfill my new life purpose: to get ever closer to my

Creator by sharing my wonderful blessings to make an extraordinary difference in the world.

A few months later, as I pondered over my life purpose and this ambitious goal, I thought, "Why not write a book to help five million people keep their promises to themselves and to the world?" I knew I could show anyone how easy it was to set goals and realize their dreams and aspirations. I also realized I could combine the book with worksheets I had developed and was using daily, to ensure long-term success. So I decided to go for it! The book would be a guide, and the worksheets would help sustain progress over time. And I could hold workshops and online seminars to help people work through their life plans in a supportive environment.

I began writing. I developed and facilitated small workshops. It was thrilling to see others' lives being changed before my eyes, simply through a new blueprint, a new way of thinking! As I wrote, I thought about some remarkable people I have been privileged to encounter on my amazing life journey. These are seemingly "ordinary" people who go about achieving extraordinary outcomes with little or no fanfare, but who keep their magnificent promises. I approached them about sharing their inspirational stories, and I am honored that they agreed to do so. I hope that their stories inspire you to keep your promises. When I shared with them the principles in this book, many of them were certain that they would have progressed much further had they been using these principles to design and manage *their* lives.

There are three reasons why this book is unique. It is the first system to help you consciously design your future using the sound principles involved in constructing complex, unique buildings. It also offers a comprehensive set of tools and perspectives with which to view and plan your life, from a unique Daily Journal that will have you seeing your days very differently, to creating an inspiring Life Vision. And it allows you to access resources to not only help you sustain but even accelerate changes over the long term.

Read the book, download the *free* workbook online at www. KeepAnyPromise.com/workbook, complete the worksheets, and learn how to define your life purpose. Using a unique and easy twelve-step process, you will set clear life goals, learn to achieve *any* goal you set, and most importantly, develop a sustainable life management system. Using this process, you will realize that you don't ever need to break a New Year's or other resolution ever again. If you read this book and complete the worksheets you will keep even your biggest promises to yourself, because this book *will* transform your life.

You will also learn about the seven magical questions you want to ask yourself each day, the twenty-year goals you will want to set for yourself, and other intriguing ways to make planning your life fun, inspiring, and purposeful. Plus you will learn how to embrace every fear you have and turn it into your ally. Above all, you will be able to implement your learnings immediately. And as a bonus, you will learn a simple way to boost your energy so you can exceed your goals.

Whether you are in your early twenties or late eighties, I have complete confidence that you, too, can keep any promise. It does not matter what your starting point is or what challenges you face at present. If you follow the simple principles outlined in this book, you *will* design a life that is breathtaking in its possibilities.

I trust that as you increasingly keep your promises, you will go through your own life transformation with this new blueprint. By letting your light illuminate the world, you will help make it a better, brighter place. There's no better time to get started than now, so join me on a journey to a world free of broken promises.

Warm wishes,

Karim H. Ismail,
Toronto, Canada
July 11, 2008

How Can You Get the Most from This Book?

Below, I suggest three options. Select one of the three and get started *today* with the material and exercises that you encounter. It does not matter which option you choose. Before you read any further, I invite you to complete the **life quiz** at <u>www.KeepAnyPromise.com/lifequiz</u>. The results may surprise you.

Option 1: If you have difficulty keeping your promises, then I invite you to start at the beginning of this book and read through the chapters, and complete the worksheets in Part 1. In Part 2, start bringing the promises and goals that you have defined into your daily life through the techniques I suggest. Once you see that achieving goals is quite easy, then you may wish to tackle the bigger life purpose questions in Part 3. Work through the book steadily and you *will* transform your life as you keep *all* your promises.

Option 2: If you already keep most promises and have a reasonable amount of success with achieving your goals, you will benefit from the techniques and tools in Part 2 to accelerate your progress. When you see yourself making huge leaps, you are ready to move on to Part 3. You will find as you complete the worksheets in Part 3 that you will likely re-evaluate your goals. As you do so, return to Part 1 to master the twelve steps to keeping *any* promise.

Option 3: If you keep all your promises and generally feel very good about your life, then start with Part 3 of the book. You will benefit tremendously from the advanced resources and tools there. As you develop what I hope will be a transformative vision for your life, come back to the start of the book and recast your goals to ensure that they resonate with your much more clearly defined purpose and life goals.

As you read the book, use the *free* workbook that you can download at www.KeepAnyPromise.com/workbook to record the answers to the many exercises in this book.

If you want to accelerate your learning and transformation, you can find details online at www.KeepAnyPromise.com about workshops and online seminars. **Be sure to use the special discount code at the end of the book to enjoy dramatically reduced pricing for yourself, your family, and friends.**

Please share your successes and challenges and any tools, tips, and tricks you have found helpful at www.KeepAnyPromise.com. I will incorporate as much as possible within the Web site and in future editions of this book.

Getting Started:

Where Are You Now and Where Do You Want to Be?

A journey of a thousand miles must begin with a single step.

—Lao-Tzu

A re you ready to begin rethinking your life? I found that the best way to get started with rethinking my life was to simply list, with brutal honesty, where I saw myself in a number of life categories today and where I wanted to see myself in three years.

Here is how I viewed the world in 2003 and how I imagined it would be in 2006.

	Life category	View of situation today (2003)	Visualization of my future (2006)
1	Financial security	Inadequate savings/growing debt/ inadequate annual income	Sound financial base; reduced business debt; doubling of annual income
2	Spirituality	Little spiritual connection	Deep spiritual connection
3	Family relationships	Strained in many instances	Happy, respectful family relationships
4	Mental outlook	Negative: little hope for the future either personally or for the human race	Highly positive, great future outlook
5	Health and fitness	Overweight, in constant, excruciating pain	At ideal weight, overcoming all back pain and other ailments
6	World impact	Little ability to make any impact on the world	Start of growing ability to impact the world
7	Happiness	Despondent	Joy-filled days

By outlining a vision of what I wanted the world to look like in the medium term, I found clarity of focus and began attracting the results I envisioned. This clarity has helped me achieve or exceed my vision handily on all the above life categories.

Now it's time to take stock of where *your* life is at today and where you would like it to be in the next three years. You may be thinking: I don't know where I want to be in three years. Don't worry. Just go through the exercise below as suggested, and I am confident that the answers will come to you, because deep down inside, your subconscious mind knows everything. You only need to exercise your imagination and get some support to bring these thoughts to the surface.

1. In Column A below, list *your* top-ten life categories, in any order you wish. Your categories can be whatever you wish: a category is simply an area of your life in which you want to constantly improve. Here are some examples of life categories, but feel free to add your own categories or to reword these:

1. Emotional outlook	11. Enduring relationships
2. Energy	12. Security
3. Financial freedom	13. Self actualization
4. Friendship	14. Self discovery
5. Fun/recreation	15. Sexual fulfillment
6. Happiness	16. Spiritual connection
7. Health/well-being	17. Time off
8. Home	18. Travel
9. Family	19. Work/career
10. Mental well-being	20. World contribution

If you cannot come up with ten categories, don't worry; list as many as you can.

2. In Column B below, be completely honest as to where you think you are *today* in every one of these categories of your life.

3. For Column C, close your eyes and think hard about the first category for one minute. What would your life be like in this category in three years if there were absolutely no obstacles in your way? Think hard and think *big*, because, as you will learn later, our minds generally react more strongly to larger visions than to small ones. Write down this vision in Column C. Write everything you can think of without editing, just like in a brainstorm exercise. Keep in mind that no idea is too big or impossible.

4. Repeat the process for each category, ensuring that you take the time to close your eyes for one minute each time, so that a wonderful vision can emerge for every category. If your vision does not make you gasp, perhaps you are not thinking big enough! The more uncomfortable and daunting the goal seems, the better.

5. For each category, rate how difficult you think attaining this vision will be in Column D. Surprisingly, you might find that even though you have a powerful vision, it may not be that difficult to actually achieve some of the results you have defined. If all of them seem very easy or easy, stop and redefine your three-year vision—you may be aiming too low.

	A	B	C	D
	Life category	My view of my world today (year):	My vision in three years (year):	Rate this from 1-5 (1 = feeling next-to-impossible 5 = feeling highly possible)
1				
2				
3				
4				
5				
6				
7				
8				
9				
10				

This worksheet is contained within the free, downloadable workbook at www.KeepAnyPromise.com/workbook.

Congratulations! You have just completed a *vital* exercise and the first step toward creating your blueprint for a fantastic life. You may be thinking: what next? How do I actually go about achieving these results and keeping my promises? You may have previously defined such results for yourself, but not achieved them. Or some of the results you have defined may seem impossible.

Don't worry, you can achieve whatever you want if you follow the step-by-step guide to achieving *any* result in the next twelve chapters. In fact, simply by thinking frequently about the three-year visions that you have outlined, you will find that results begin to appear in your life, slowly but surely. Quite simply, this is the Law of Attraction at work, proposed by James Allen in 1902 in *As a Man Thinketh*. He wrote, "The soul attracts that which it secretly harbors, that which it loves, and also that which it fears. It reaches the height of its cherished aspirations. It falls to the level of its unchastened desires—and circumstances are the means by which the soul receives its own."

PART 1:
How Can I Get There?

The tragedy of life doesn't lie in not reaching your goal. The tragedy lies in having no goals to reach.

—*Benjamin Mays*

In the next twelve chapters, you will have the opportunity to take one of your three-year results and learn a technique that you can use to achieve *any* goal, in twelve easy strides. Why is it important to achieve your goals? Simply because doing so will help you keep the promises you make to yourself, your family, and the world. Your goals therefore are a key part of keeping the big promises you will make all your life.

What is a goal? It is simply an intended result or outcome. That's it. Because you have just defined up to ten results (otherwise known as goals) for your life over the next three years, you are already a goal-setter!

In the next twelve chapters, you will encounter twelve wonderful people who will inspire you as you take each stride. I am blessed to know these people of all ages, from all walks of life. Their stories, collectively, illustrate that each of us can achieve this level (or higher) of greatness, especially if we think through and plan out our lives. They are proof that "ordinary" people like you and I can achieve extraordinary things, simply by thinking and acting on our thoughts.

The most important part of this section is the time and thinking *you* put into the short exercise at the end of each chapter. Each chapter builds on the theme of the previous one, so go step by step. At the end of the twelve chapters, you will be able to summarize all your thoughts. I guarantee that you will be amazed by your own thinking and how easy it is to set and achieve huge goals.

Keep in mind that you can actually write out the exercises in the book, but you might find it a lot easier and quicker to simply download the Achieve *Any* Goal worksheet from www.KeepAnyPromise.com/workbook to use instead.

Either way, let's roll up our sleeves and get started.

Chapter 1:

What Is Your Most Important and *Audacious* Goal?

The boundary of your dreams is the measure of your success.
Dare to dream.

—*Elma Easley*

When thinking about the results or goals you want to achieve, start by focusing on those goals that have the most meaning to you. Think of those achievements from which you have the most to gain. You will discover a simple truth: our minds do not change their deeply-ingrained ways of thinking if we set *small* goals.

Here's an example. Say you want to lose weight. If you set a small goal of five to ten pounds, you will likely make some progress. But your mind does not have to *think* differently. Now suppose you had an audacious goal? Like losing forty pounds or more and keeping the weight off permanently? Your mind needs to engage on a *different* level. It knows that tinkering with food choices, exercise, etc., is not the answer. Something needs to change in a drastic way. Indeed, significant lifestyle changes are needed.

Keep in mind that no matter how large your goal, you will be achieving it in small chunks. But the act of setting large, seemingly impossible goals spurs your mind to think differently. And thinking differently is key to achieving your goal, because after all, it's your current thinking that has landed you where you are today.

3

Let me illustrate this point about setting huge goals with the example of my friend Audrey Loeb, the founder of the highly successful Weekend to End Breast Cancer 60km Walk.

Audrey's Story and Her Promise

"It all began in February 2002 when I was on a hiking holiday in Utah. I met two sisters who invited me to join them in Chicago in June 2002 to undertake a three-day, sixty-mile walk called the Avon Three-Day. The invitation was intriguing. Lots of training meant I was bound to lose weight. It was a great personal challenge for a cause I really care about, given my sister's personal brush with cancer. And I wondered: could this be a new idea for funding for the Princess Margaret Hospital Foundation, where I was a board member for the past six years?

"So I invited my good friend, Gloria, whose sister had died of breast cancer, to join me. She jumped at the chance to participate in the sixty-mile walk so that we could understand the many challenges involved. While I was a regular walker, the thought of doing sixty miles was daunting, but I dutifully started training.

"In June 2002, over three days with thousands of women and men, we walked, talked, laughed, and cried a lot, and we had the time of our lives. It was one of the great experiences of my life. I never thought I could complete sixty miles! But the wonderful spirit of the event and the knowledge of how completing the walk could help others kept us going.

"Complete the walk we did, even though we had blisters, were sore, and exhausted. We were also elated. We then worked diligently to deliver our plans. We decided that if we were going to do a breast cancer fundraiser walk in Canada, we should keep it to sixty kilometers, over two days, not three days, so that the walk was accessible to many more people and avoided work time conflicts. We named it the Weekend to End Breast Cancer.

"When I got home from Chicago, I talked about nothing else. I immediately spoke to our board chairman, Lionel Robbins, and our president,

Neville Kirchmann, and got the go-ahead to investigate the possibility of doing a similar event in Toronto for the Princess Margaret Hospital Foundation. I contacted the company that ran the U.S. event and started discussions. After an initial encouraging response, they stopped communicating with us. It turned out they were filing for bankruptcy.

"We made contact with two of their employees. After much investigation and soul searching, we took a huge gamble and hired them to help us. No one in Canada knew about this type of event. We had to make the public aware of the event and interested in doing it. We needed to spend money and lots of it, buying airtime on radio and TV; printing materials to respond to inquiries and explain the event; and staff to support all this. We were looking at spending $1.4 million before knowing if the event would even proceed. Even I began to have some doubts as to whether this audacious feat could be pulled off.

"Neville and I finalized the details and presented it to the board in November 2002. We had strong support, but this was not a 'done deal.' Board members had concerns. There were no major sponsors to defray the upfront costs. Sixty kilometers over two days was too difficult. Fundraising a minimum of $2,000 per walker was too onerous. The impact our event might have on other breast cancer fundraising events run by different agencies was unclear. It was all too fast. We needed more time to try to get sponsorships and investigate it all more thoroughly.

"The board asked many more questions, but after thorough due diligence, they unanimously approved the event. I remember looking at Lionel just before the board voted and thinking, 'Oh my goodness, what have I done? I hope I am right about this.' Our first radio ad aired in the second week of January 2003, just seven months after I returned from Chicago. For the next six months, the weekend became the focus of our Weekend to End Breast Cancer Committee.

"The day we hit break-even in terms of registrants was one of great relief, especially as Toronto faced the SARS outbreak, a very cold winter, a power blackout that impacted the entire East Coast, and the threat of a postal strike. But people registered; teams formed and started raising money, often more than the required minimum. Excitement started to build.

"We led training walks, hosted orientations for walkers, formed teams, and talked to everyone we could about becoming involved. However, the real reason for success was the walkers. As they became engaged, our results improved. People devised all kinds of ways to raise money. From standing outside beer stores to tell their stories, to selling hot dogs at grocery stores, to holding garage sales and bake sales. One team actually hosted a carnival. The Weekend empowered its participants. It fulfilled their need to make a difference and let them be part of something that was bigger than any one person.

"As the event drew closer, we knew we had created something wonderful. It was everything we hoped it would be and more. The first Weekend to End Breast Cancer walk in 2003 in Toronto attracted 3,972 walkers, 300 crew, 340 volunteers, and 150,000 individual donors. We raised $12.6 million for the treatment, education, and research of breast cancer. From every perspective, it was a hit. And in 2007, the walk took take place in seven cities, coast to coast, attracted 15,670 walkers, involved almost 400,000 individual donors, and raised $44.8 million countrywide for the fight against breast cancer. The total we've raised for the Princess Margaret Hospital in five years is $78.5 million and for hospitals across the country, $144 million."

Lessons

Audrey's amazing story illustrates in a very simple way that having a bold goal, and acting on it, can yield incredible results, even if one is plagued with uncertainty at the start. While the above results are impressive in themselves, Audrey has so far completed six walks and raised $100,000 herself. But her accomplishments go far beyond the number of people walking or funds raised. She has helped countless people improve their fitness and confidence levels. Audrey has helped people who never thought they could raise money for any cause to do so. And she has given hope and encouragement to breast cancer survivors, patients, and their families, who now know that so many thousands of people care deeply enough to get together and walk sixty kilometers because they all want to help eliminate this dreadful and often fatal disease. Above all, she has dramatically increased public awareness about breast cancer.

I am deeply honored to know Audrey Loeb, a real estate lawyer, fundraiser, and life-changer extraordinaire, to whom I am extremely grateful for helping me develop the confidence to completely turn my life around through my participation in the walk she helped launch. Audrey exemplifies the ability we each have, to set and achieve truly audacious goals, for ourselves and for others.

➲ Now, It's Your Turn

So, let's begin by picking one of the life categories that you listed earlier. Pick one that is the most important to you and simply rewrite below, or on the worksheet you downloaded from www.KeepAnyPromise.com, where you would like to be in three years in this category. You will eventually have the opportunity to go through the same thinking process for all your life categories.

_____

_____

_____

_____

_____

If you took this important first step, bravo! You have begun your journey of goal achievement with the simple task of stating a huge goal, which

I hope seems challenging to you. The more uncomfortable and daunting it seems, the better. I'll say it again: *the more uncomfortable and daunting it seems, the better.* In other words ... if it doesn't cause discomfort, it's not a big enough goal, so aim higher.

In Chapter 2, you will learn why it is important to define a clear time-frame for your goal.

Chapter 2:
What Is Your Timeframe?

A goal is a dream with a plan and a deadline.

—*Harvey Mackay*

Think about a time in your life when you had a deadline. Perhaps before leaving for a trip, handing in a school assignment, or completing a project at work? You were likely extremely focused when you had a deadline. Likewise, it is important to define a deadline or timeframe for achieving your goal. I highly recommend a three-year timeframe for a *huge* goal. But go with whatever timeframe your instinct signals to you.

There is another vital reason for defining a deadline. A deadline is key to defining milestones along the path to your goals, which allows you to chunk up your goal into manageable parts. You will learn more about milestones in Chapter 10.

Allow me to share with you the story of my eleven-year-old nephew, Bilaal Rajan, and how external deadlines have shaped his life. Bilaal has been fundraising for charities for seven years.

Bilaal's Story and His Promise

"I started wanting to help people (and still do) when I was just four years old. My parents told me about the suffering of the people in Gujarat, India, when a massive earthquake struck there. I wanted to help, and since I was eating a mandarin orange at that time, I told my parents that I should start selling these door-to-door to raise money to send to Gujarat. I used up my piggy bank money and went out and sold $350 worth of oranges to residents in my neighborhood.

"Then in September 2004, a UNICEF plea in the newspaper for help for victims of the devastating hurricanes in Haiti with a crying child's picture motivated me to get involved. I asked my father if I could sell boxes of cookies his company distributes to schools. My father thought that I would only sell fifteen to twenty boxes, but with my team of other schoolmates and friends, we went on to sell over a thousand boxes.

"At first, my parents and I were the only ones who believed that I could make a difference. But slowly, with persistence and determination, I won over people's hearts and support. It was hard to get other team members motivated to sell the cookies and to get more people to help. But the cookies kept selling, and everyone was surprised that I did not want to give up.

"I knew that the children of Haiti needed more than just the money we were fundraising. That's when I thought of calling companies to donate products instead of money. I was amazed at the response: over $500,000 worth of food, medicine, and supplies were donated. After the crisis in Haiti, I didn't stop. I hand-made acrylic plates (initially for my teachers' Christmas gifts) that I sold to the public, even outside the main train station in the freezing cold, in support of AIDS victims.

"Then the tsunami struck in Southeast Asia in December 2004. I knew I had to act quickly because help was need urgently. I started contacting everyone I knew, but I felt it was not enough. I contacted UNICEF Canada days after the disaster to raise more funds in order to help children and their families in need.

"Together we initiated the Canada Kids Earthquake Challenge, where I challenged every child in Canada to personally raise $100 for this cause, with a minimum of $1 million being the total goal. The Canadian public, including major school boards, responded quickly, and with matching government support, I estimate this initiative raised over $4 million.

"I ate, slept, and breathed fundraising for tsunami victims. I gave talks at schools, made cold calls to companies, sold hand-made arts and crafts, spearheaded special events, and even created my own Web site. And managed to personally raise $50,000 for children affected by the tsunami.

"But I wanted to do more. I wanted to see first-hand not only the damage caused by the tsunami, but also the support extended, and the goodwill and restoration being done with the funds we, across Canada, had raised. I asked my parents and UNICEF Canada if I could visit the countries worst affected by the tsunami. I was overjoyed when they agreed. The trip was very tiring, but it made me very happy to see the difference our funds and supplies were making in the lives of other children.

"I believe that there is good in all children to help in whatever way to make a difference in the world. I believe that there should be equality and fairness in the world for all children. I know that together, we can make a difference!"

Lessons

The tight deadlines for each of the disaster relief efforts helped Bilaal focus his efforts so that he could reach his ambitious goals. Bilaal has since gone on to raise millions to help children around the world and is a UNICEF Canada National Child Ambassador, the youngest in the world. He was also honored in June 2008 with Youth in Motion's Top 20 under 20 award for 2008, an incredible honor given his age. No one I know can help but be touched by the compassion in such a young child. How he manages to juggle a heavy school and extracurricular activity schedule with interviews, travel, and fundraising remains a mystery to me. Please see the references section at www.KeepAnyPromise.com for more details on Bilaal, his accomplishments and current projects.

I share his story not only for his wonderful efforts, but because of the lesson he taught me. When I decided to fundraise for the Weekend to End Breast Cancer 60km walk, I was unsure of the support I would receive, as it had been thirty years since I had fundraised. But seeing the results of a then-eight-year-old's efforts convinced me that while I am not as cute as he is, if he could do it, so could I. Bilaal's complete lack of fear in asking for donations became the role model I followed, and people have been most generous in their support in all my endeavors to date.

⮡ Now, It's Your Turn

Think about your timeframe or deadline for achieving your huge, outrageous goal, and then write it below or in the worksheet you downloaded. While in most cases this will be a three-year timeframe for a huge goal, let your instinct guide your timeframe, making it either less or more than three years.

_____

_____

_____

_____

_____

Chapter 3:

How Will You Measure It?

Start by doing what's necessary, then what's possible, and suddenly you are doing the impossible.

—*Saint Francis of Assisi*

For some goals, it is easy to define how you will measure progress. For example, if your goal was to "lose weight and get fitter," you could measure weight loss, your Body Mass Index, the distance you can easily walk or run in a given time, etc. These are very concrete ways to measure weight loss and fitness gain.

If your goal was "improved family relationships," it is more difficult to measure progress. But if you try hard, anything can be measured. Sometimes, you may have to define a whole set of "soft" performance measures to give you a good way to assess your progress. In this example, is the frequency of family contact increased, especially if there is geographical distance between family members? Are the interactions deeper and more meaningful and satisfying? Are you increasingly happy emerging from those interactions? One way or the other, each of your goals can and should be measured, or you will never know whether you are making progress or have met your goals.

Below is the story of my friend Frank Tielve, whose therapy quite simply saved my life in 2002 when I had debilitating back pain. Through his help, I was able to regain my life and avoid major back surgery, for which I will always be deeply grateful. Frank's story illustrates how important it is to have clear, measurable goals.

Frank's Story and His Promise

"Growing up as a teenager in Vancouver, I witnessed my father struggle with back pain at the young age of forty-one. For a couple of years, he tried every form of therapy available, and despite some slight improvement from time to time, his back and overall health declined rapidly. He resorted to back surgery to fuse his vertebrae, and his health declined further. Indeed, he was to never recover his former good health.

"At about the same time, my parents had a young tenant family in an apartment they rented out. The young man was thirty-three and very slightly overweight, but otherwise in great health. He started having back problems; they got really worse. Conventional medicine could not help him, so he too went for surgery. Except he never returned home from the surgery, for it took his life.

"These incidents left an indelible mark on me as I was growing up, but the memories began to fade until I experienced severe back pain myself some twenty years ago in 1987, in my thirties. I had seen the devastating impact of conventional medical and other therapies, so I wanted to avoid conventional therapies at any cost.

"I began studying the human anatomy to determine the root cause of back issues, and over the next two years began developing a system that I used to dramatically improve my back condition. I was also at a turning point in my life, and I was looking for a project that I could do independently, so with my initial success, I set about opening a clinic so I could help other people. The memories of my father's struggles and the tenant's death, coupled with my own struggles and then success, gave me the fortitude I needed to defy the medical/health care establishment and offer a radically different alternative, long before alternative therapies were as common as they are today.

"As I helped other people overcome their back problems, I continued my research and refined my techniques. Before long, I was running a number of clinics, helping many people. My early research into the effective treatment of back pain and sciatica led to my discovery that there are dozens of health problems that originate in an unfit spine, for example: hair loss, osteoarthritis, migraine headaches, high blood pressure, hemorrhoids, carpal tunnel syndrome, chronic constipation, bursitis, etc. In fact, so many ailments are caused by an unfit spine that my research is now directed at finding health ailments that are not somehow related to the unfit spine—so far, I cannot identify any!

"I continued my research, and soon I had developed a methodology that I could confidently use to cure back pain in ten days, while also relieving many other symptoms. This was all the more remarkable because many of the patients I saw had suffered extreme back pain for many years, just as Karim had. Others were post-surgical patients, some with multiple unsuccessful surgeries. Many were 'lost causes,' condemned to living out their lives in excruciating pain, with little hope for improvement.

"But no matter how much I tried, I was unable to train others to learn and successfully execute the techniques I had developed. They just could not duplicate my treatment results, as they lacked the natural unique sensing mechanism that I have in my right hand. Without that unique information feedback mechanism, another therapist has absolutely no knowledge of the existing condition or control of the treatment process and therefore could not achieve the required changes.

"So I renewed my research and soon developed a treatment program that the patient could use at home after a few initial training sessions. Success gave me the confidence that I would be able to replicate my methodologies to treat hundreds of thousands, even millions of people simultaneously, something that had eluded me to date.

"I hope to use my additional research into the previously unknown connections between an unfit spine and almost every health problem that humans suffer to revolutionize health care worldwide, since I am convinced that today's medical treatment procedures target symptoms without a good understanding of their true origin or hope of a permanent cure.

"I decided therefore to open a series of wellness clinics. The first Saludex Health Studio to offer the new system opened to the general public in April 2008 in Toronto. The role of the Saludex Health Studio franchises will be to spread worldwide the new Transmodular Physical Science knowledge I have developed, and to empower the common person to preserve or regain their former health by using simple, cost-effective tools and do-it-yourself techniques.

"It is my goal over the next twenty years to open thousands of additional health studios worldwide through a franchise system, at a rate of four hundred to five hundred per year. This may sound like a lot, but keep in mind that McDonalds started in 1955 with a single franchise, and just five decades later, it is the largest and most recognized brand in the world, with more than thirty thousand restaurants in a hundred and twenty countries. Given the tremendous health care benefits Saludex will offer, I am confident that I can achieve my goal of opening at least eight thousand new franchises in twenty years.

"During that time, I intend to eliminate back pain for more than eight hundred million people worldwide, increasing their longevity by more than 20 percent and reducing their morbidity by 80 percent. Every patient's progress will be carefully tracked, from when he or she first enrolls.

"I know that by continuing my research into the mysteries of the human body, and especially the spine, I will continually improve and refine my techniques, so as to be able to offer even greater help for millions around the world. Knowledge is power, and the preservation of our health is our own responsibility, so I intend to empower millions to regain control over their health."

Lessons

Frank's example shows us how important it is to set a measurable goal. After his initial success treating himself and others at his clinics, he could simply have stopped. But knowing that he wanted to help millions of people led him to continually research and develop new treatment modalities, until he found a system that can help millions of people relieve not just back problems, but also improve their overall health.

➲ Now, It's Your Turn

Define below or on the worksheet you downloaded how you will measure your goal. Be as specific as you can.

_____

_____

_____

_____

_____

Chapter 4:

What Are Your Compelling Reasons?

Strong reasons make strong actions.

—*William Shakespeare*

I f you cannot articulate a clear, compelling reason for why you *must* achieve a goal, especially a huge goal, you will likely not achieve your goal. Why? Simply because achieving any goal will likely involve changes in your life. It will possibly take you out of your comfort zone. It will most likely challenge your thinking. It may require hard work. So unless you have compelling and powerful reasons for why it is important for you to achieve your goal, you significantly diminish your chances of achievement.

One of the people who best exemplifies the concept of how a compelling reason can propel one to achieve one's goal is my uncle, Alli Amlani. I have known Alli since he married my aunt Nasim when I was thirteen.

Alli's Story and His Promise

"1976 to 1980 were tumultuous years for Nasim and I. We had just moved to Canada, had to settle for low paying jobs, and had to adjust to a different way of life. We had less than $500 in our pockets because that was all we were allowed to transfer out of Kenya, due to strict foreign exchange controls.

"None of our previous experience or skills were recognized in Canada. I was told I lacked Canadian experience or was 'overqualified' for the job. But somehow we knew that we had made the right decision in uprooting ourselves and moving to Canada. We were determined, knew that we had each other's support, and were well prepared for the challenges that lay ahead. Making a new life for ourselves and the children that followed gave us a compelling reason for hanging in, through thick and thin.

"Soon we learned that Nasim was pregnant, at age thirty-two. We were overjoyed, because after almost eight years of a happy but childless marriage, we had just about given up hope of ever having our own child. Many of the options available to couples today were not available then.

"On July 9, 1977, our child was born prematurely at three and a half pounds, and she shrank to under three pounds very shortly after birth. Aliza was very ill, and with little hope of survival she was rushed to an incubator at the Hospital for Sick Children, Toronto, while Nasim recovered from a complex caesarean section.

"Aliza stayed in hospital for over six weeks, gaining a little less than an ounce a day before getting to the safe level of five pounds, when we could bring her home. Our faith in Canada and in God was reinforced. And in less than a month after Aliza came home, my seventeen-year-old nephew, Karim, arrived in Canada to live with us to complete his pre-university year of high school.

"Although it was a difficult time, as we struggled to make ends meet, it was also the most gratifying and eventful time in our lives. Being overjoyed is an understatement as we reflect back to our beginnings in our new land. It was also an opportunity to fulfill an old promise I had made to myself in my younger days. Back then, due to the financial constraints my family faced, I was unable to continue further education, although I had the opportunity to do so. I made a commitment that I would do all I could in my power to ensure that others would not face the same fate that I had without a solid education—namely, many doors being closed to me and having to work much harder to make career progress.

"Getting into the teaching profession enabled me to make some contribution to this plight, but I felt it was inadequate. In 1966, an opportunity arose to help my sister-in-law Nargis, who was orphaned at six. I became her guardian, had her come and live with us in Nairobi from Mombasa, saw her though her grade school education, and supported her while she earned a Degree in Fine Arts from the University of Nairobi. I was overjoyed at being able to help the first member of our family to get a university education.

"The next opportunity we had was when Karim came to live with us in Canada. He would be the first male in our family to go to university, and there was no price too big to pay to get him there. Karim had two aunts, eight years and three years older than him, who were very close to him and were great role models, one of whom was Nargis. They acquired a university education and subsequently graduated with honors.

"During the year with us, Karim showed amazing focus at school, where he coped with many unfamiliar subjects, was a big help with Aliza, and enriched our lives, notwithstanding normal nuisances: sleeping in or watching television late at night, especially on weekends.

"I supplemented our incomes by obtaining a cabdriver's license, a grueling six-month training experience on a part-time basis. I drove mainly on weekends, sometimes pulling off double shifts. It was the stuff that builds character: the memory of the challenges we overcame has sustained us through many tribulations over the years.

"After changing jobs, I ventured into my own business, expanded, and then diversified. By this time, we had moved into a new home of our own.

"In 1987, I took ill and could no longer continue with my business, as it was physically demanding. A close friend offered me a job in his immigration law firm on a profit-sharing basis. I jumped at the chance because in addition to the income opportunity, I knew I would impact the lives of many people and their families and help them achieve their goals.

"By January 1988, I was working for the law firm in Korea. I managed immigration applications from people anxious to settle in Canada or to be reunited with family in Canada. It was gratifying work.

"However, I cherished my independence, so I soon left to set up my own immigration consulting practice. My competition was the many legal firms and other consultants, some rather unethical. But I was determined to provide excellent service at a fair price, but only when I achieved success for clients.

"The company, Interconnections Canada, grew on these principles. We had established fourteen offices in twelve countries by 1992. My spouse Nasim quit her administrative job at an oil company to join our international staff of forty-one, to help me with a growing caseload.

"Some of the cases we dealt with were complex. Long processing timeframes and a deep emotional impact on families, due to long-drawn processes and appeals with government agencies, created trauma for many. But I was compelled to do my best for our clients, because I knew that Canada had tremendous potential, and it would benefit greatly from the many hard-working and self-sacrificing individuals and families who move here every year. I prepared them mentally for short-term pain but long-term gain, citing my own example.

"We have been fortunate to have been able to help over twenty thousand people meet their aspirations and successfully establish themselves in Canada. Drawing from my early experiences, we have expanded our services to ensure that we offer a comprehensive resettlement service, now in four major cities in Canada. This includes temporary-to-permanent accommodation, government registrations, admission to schools, and introductions to banks and other associations and institutions. Above all, it also includes help with getting a new job or setting up a new business. The memories of being told we had 'inadequate Canadian experience' or were 'overqualified' are compelling reasons for the extra services we offer through a placement agency we also began.

"Every year we held a party to welcome new immigrants and to create a networking opportunity with more established immigrants. Members of Parliament and ministers attended to welcome these newcomers.

"I am humbled at the opportunity that has been given to me to help so many people over the last twenty years. I am also delighted that our daughter Aliza has contributed immensely as a part-time education consultant to help many of our clients' children meet their educational and career goals.

"In addition to working with our clients, I also wanted to raise the profile and reputation of our profession. Joining a newly-formed Association of Professional Immigration Consultants and volunteering my time resulted in my becoming a member of the board of directors over a ten-year period. During that time, we initiated educational programs for our members with the Government of Canada. We developed an Immigration Practitioners Certificate Program in conjunction with Seneca College of Applied Arts and Technology and York University. Today, this program is also being delivered at the University of British Columbia and Bow Valley College in Alberta. We also fought hard for self regulation and tougher practice standards, which finally materialized in early 2004."

Lessons

Alli's example shows us that, given the adversities he had to face along the way, had it not been for the compelling goals he and his wife Nasim set for themselves, first to adapt successfully to their new land, and second, when the opportunity arose, to help many families through their immigration consulting practice, he would likely have given up many times over the years. What is even more heartening is that Alli is President of the Ontario Chapter of CAPIC (the Canadian Association of Professional Immigration Consultants), in the second year of a four-year term. This role helps him make a significant contribution to immigration in Canada.

And on a very personal note, my life would have likely turned out very differently had Alli and Nasim not felt compelled to make huge sacrifices in order for me to get a great education in Canada. I am deeply grateful.

➲ Now, It's Your Turn

Define below or on the worksheet you downloaded, *your* absolutely compelling reasons for achieving your goal. Focus on *why* it's really important to you to achieve this goal. Your reasons could stem from a huge challenge, from your pain, someone else's pain, an image, etc. Think hard, and make these reasons as emotional as possible, as we are all driven by our emotions, no matter how rational we think we are. Be careful not to focus on benefits in this section, as we will deal with benefits in the next chapter. Instead simply list *why* it's important to achieve this result.

_____

_____

_____

_____

_____

Chapter 5:

What Benefits Do You Expect to Gain?

Opportunities? They are all around us. … There is power living latent everywhere waiting for the observant eye to discover it.

—*Orison Swett Marden*

Once you define the key benefits or results you expect, you will be more driven to do what it takes to achieve your goal. Make this list as detailed as possible: the more benefits to be gained, the greater the focus you will have on the goal.

Below is the story of my close friend and role model, Aziz M. Bhaloo. I have known Aziz for over twenty-five years during which our paths crossed on many volunteer committees, boards, and projects. Aziz's example shows us that setting and monitoring goals results in many benefits, often far greater than we could have imagined when we first envisioned our goal.

Aziz's Story and His Promise

"I was born and educated in Kenya and immigrated to Canada in 1974 from Nairobi in search of a better future for our family: my wife, Amina, and two children, Azam and Ambreen, who were then five and three years old. Amina, who had been a high school vice-principal and had run a highly successful early childhood education center in Nairobi, decided to start her own daycare service in Canada out of necessity.

"While the early years were difficult, and along the way there were many swings in government regulations that caused us to wonder whether our growing business would survive, today, with God's grace, we have expanded to nine centers, with about a thousand children, and private schools and a food service company serving children in childcare centers and schools.

"The benefits we have seen from this growth have been the ability to provide high-quality early childhood education to over twenty thousand young children over the years so that they get a great start in life, at a fair price, while also offering fulfilling careers and long-term employment to the two hundred and fifty staff we currently employ. Azam now runs the business, having qualified as a chartered accountant and obtaining an MBA from the University of Toronto. He is assisted by Ambreen, who has a Master's in Administration from the University of Pennsylvania, and a team of professional managers.

"I graduated as an engineer, but moved on to various management roles at Esso, first in Kenya and then in Canada. But I quickly learned that if I wanted to have the kind of future I desired, I would have to become an entrepreneur. My overarching goal was to spend more time with my children and on long-term wealth creation, while also having increasing amounts of time to volunteer for the betterment of my community and country. Volunteerism had been ingrained in me since my childhood days, and I had a wonderful role model in my mother, who had volunteered for many causes.

"My first venture was in printing. Since then I have been involved in real estate investments and plastics manufacturing, among other ventures. Each of these businesses has, with God's grace, thrived, and I am able to monitor them closely while most times playing a strategic, non-operational role.

"Along the way, I developed a strong ability to set big goals, to monitor these goals closely, and to define the benefits that I expected to get. I have found that these skills have been invaluable in both my business ventures and in my volunteer activities. Indeed, one of the key benefits of being able to operate a number of businesses at a strategic level has been that it has left me time to spend on volunteer activities for my faith-based community. Over the last almost forty years, I have been blessed to be involved in the areas of communication and media, education, emergency relief, third-world development, and in overseeing the affairs of the Ismaili Muslim community in Canada as president of its governing body for six years. My ability to render volunteer service has been the biggest benefit from achieving my goal.

"I am deeply grateful to be the current chairman of FOCUS International Coordination Committee, which oversees the efforts of FOCUS Humanitarian Assistance, an international non-profit with offices in Europe, North America, and South Asia. FOCUS is an international emergency response agency providing humanitarian relief and assistance and disaster risk management for vulnerable communities located primarily in the developing world.

"In 2007, I was very gratified to be asked to assume a diplomatic position as resident representative in Kenya of the Aga Khan Development Network, the world's second-largest development agency after the Ford Foundation. You see, I left Kenya in 1974, never thinking I would return to my ancestral homeland. Though we have very strong roots in Canada, we have taken on the challenge of leaving behind family, including our granddaughters, and many close friends, to move to Kenya, in the hope that the experience and wisdom we have gained over the last forty-plus years can be used to help improve the lives of thousands of people through the work of the Aga Khan Development Network in Kenya."

Lessons

Aziz's clear definition of the benefits that he would attain from reaching his goal painted for him a vision that sustained him during many difficult times. His blessing is that not only did he end up achieving the benefits he had targeted, but he has been able to help many other less privileged members of society.

Getting clear about the benefits of achieving your goal is therefore critical to keeping your promises.

➲ Now, It's Your Turn

List as specifically as possible below, or in the workbook you downloaded, the key benefits you expect from reaching your goal. List as many benefits as possible.

1.	
2.	
3.	
4.	
5.	
6.	
7.	
8.	
9.	
10.	

Chapter 6:

What Are the Consequences of *Not* Achieving Your Goal?

Our greatest glory is not in never failing but in rising every time we fall.

—*Confucius*

T he psychologist Sigmund Freud observed that that the human mind is consciously and subconsciously motivated by two forces: the need to avoid pain and the need to gain pleasure. Pain is often more immediate than pleasure, so we may become more concerned with avoiding pain and, in general, develop a preference towards avoidance.

So it is important to define with clarity the consequences of not achieving your goal. Put another way, what is the pain that will result from not achieving your goal? As you define these consequences, you will be motivated to avoid this pain and to focus on your goal, especially if you have also clearly outlined the *benefits* of achieving it.

Here is the story of my good friend Nilofer Juma. Her story exemplifies how, when her life circumstances changed dramatically, she was able to overcome numerous obstacles, because the consequences of not doing

---

* The names and some details in this story have been changed to protect the family's privacy.

so would have been too difficult to bear. In other words, she was highly motivated to avoid pain.

Nilofer's Story and Her Promise

"I grew up in Jinja, Uganda, and in my late teens was forced to flee Uganda when then-President Idi Amin expelled all Asians, giving them ninety days to leave the country, even though many of us were second-generation Ugandans with Ugandan citizenship. Overnight, we were stateless! It was a frightening and bewildering experience.

"I arrived with only my older sister in Toronto in the fall of 1972. My parents owned a business in Uganda, and during our transit through Europe, they decided to settle in London, England, and start all over again, which they managed to do by working extremely hard.

"I was too late to register for university, so I took some community college courses for a year and then enrolled in the Arts and Science program at York University, Toronto, with a concentration in psychology. I especially enjoyed my child-oriented developmental psychology classes, so I decided to specialize in child developmental psychology at the graduate level.

"I was immediately able to find work in my selected field and very much enjoyed working with children who had learning disabilities, some minor, some very severe. My then-fiancé and I decided to get married a couple of years after I graduated. I had met him at York University, and we fell deeply in love. Sadiq was a math wizard and was keen to become an actuary.

"Our early years were blissful, and two years later, our daughter, Aziza, was born. We loved her very much, and decided to have a second child. While the second pregnancy was as normal as the first one, there were complications during labor, and our son was deprived of oxygen long enough to cause brain damage, we discovered later. A few minutes at birth were to change our family's life completely, something I could never have predicted.

"While Hanif seemed normal to everyone, including our pediatrician, my training made me wonder whether he was not experiencing developmental challenges. The pediatrician dismissed my concerns as being those of an 'overeducated mother.'

"At five months, Hanif had convulsions in my arms while I was nursing him. We rushed him to the Hospital for Sick Children, Toronto, and very quickly, the doctors there confirmed that he had been having seizures for at least the past twenty-four hours. They soon pieced together what had happened at birth, which was the cause of the seizures. They prescribed strong medication that helped control his seizures. They also broke the news that he would likely have a permanent developmental delay.

"At first, Sadiq and I were devastated with the news. We were very grateful, however, that our son was alive and stabilized, and we knew we would love him just as much as we loved Aziza, a precocious three-year-old by then.

"It then hit me like a thunderbolt. While I had many career choices, there was surely a divine force that made me want to study developmental psychology and provide me with the perfect educational background and some experience in working with developmentally handicapped children.

"Sadiq was quite supportive at first, with both children. He was completing his actuarial exams and working full time, so we decided I would not return to work, but look after Hanif until he was older and we could assess how much ongoing care he needed.

"This was a stressful period, especially as Hanif had to be hospitalized for long periods, followed by his coming home, and soon, back to the hospital. I thought we were coping quite well, but I was mistaken, as it turns out, for the strain proved to be too much for Sadiq.

"One morning, out of the blue, he announced to me that he wanted to separate and start a new life—at the other end of the country in Vancouver—with someone he had met, as it turns out, at the hospital. I was shattered, because I still loved him very much, but he was adamant that he wanted to separate. He indicated that he would do everything he could to support the children financially, and he would try and see them as best he could as they were growing up.

"So here I was, in Toronto, at thirty-two, with two children: a lovely four-and-a-half-year-old daughter and an equally lovely two-year-old son who needed constant care, as his development lagged consistently. I knew that I would have to be very strong, because if I could not provide my son with the care I knew he would need, he would end up either hospitalized for long periods or in a group home, away from family. The consequences of my not being able to care for him were too painful to even think about. I vowed never to let this happen, no matter what sacrifices I had to make.

"My parents, who had settled in London, England, could not be much help, as their business was finally showing signs of promise. Starting from scratch once again in Canada would have been too much for them. So I encouraged them to stay in London, downplaying the amount of care that Hanif needed. My older sister and her husband were the only other family I had in Toronto, and they have been a godsend, going way beyond the call of duty to be supportive.

"In those first years, until Hanif turned five, I could not work, as I was his full-time caregiver. Sadiq's financial support, along with that from my sister's family, was crucial to my being able to take full-time care of Hanif. Aziza was also becoming difficult to manage from time to time, likely resenting the large amounts of time I had to spend with Hanif. I did whatever I could to set aside special time for her, for I loved her as much as I loved Hanif.

"I thought long and hard about the turn of events in my life, and slowly it dawned on me that I was indeed blessed. I felt blessed that I was healthy, that I had one very healthy child, and that God had steered me towards getting the exact training and preparation that I would need to care for my son. But most of all, I felt blessed at having been chosen to look after Hanif. I resolved to do my best.

"By age six, Hanif was relatively stable, and I was able to place him with other children in a segregated setting that would meet his needs appropriately. I was also able to work in the same center, and soon he started school, albeit at a much slower pace than other children.

"However, by the time he was thirteen, he was having great difficulty coping at school and becoming very difficult to manage. The centre could no longer meet his needs, and I had to pull him out of school and quit the work I loved doing. I was heartbroken at not being able to help the other children who I had grown to love at the school, but again, I reminded myself of the consequences of not being able to look after Hanif. I knew what I had to do, for I did not want to give up having him at home.

"For the next few years, Hanif stayed home with me, and gradually we found the right combination of therapies, activities, and medication to allow him to stabilize and mature into a loving, caring, and gentle adult.

"Meanwhile, there were other consequences I had to cope with. Aziza and I had an increasingly tumultuous relationship, and she left home at eighteen to begin at McGill University in Montreal. After some initial adjustments, she settled down, and she recently graduated with straight A's. At first, Aziza rarely returned home during her breaks, but in her later years, she would come home every chance she could and help me with Hanif. Our relationship went from being a difficult one to a great friendship, as she learned that I loved her every bit as much as Hanif, something she could not see clearly when she was growing up.

"As for Sadiq, he kept his word and provided financial support until the children were adults. Gradually, though, he stopped seeing them, so the children missed out on having a father. My parents eventually wound down their business in the UK, and they moved to Toronto a few years ago. We live together now, having been separated for far too long. My elder sister, my brother-in-law, and their three children have been a wonderful support, for which I am deeply grateful.

"As I look back over the years, I feel very blessed at having Aziza and Hanif in my life. I am also grateful at the preparation I received in working with children. Had I not had this background, as much as I love children, I don't believe I would have felt capable of caring for Hanif on my own, especially knowing I had God's watchful eye over me; I would have likely considered placing Hanif in a group home, to be cared for by external caregivers.

I am certain that the consequences of doing so would have been that Hanif would still have near-insurmountable developmental challenges. I know I would not have achieved the same remarkable results I have with Hanif, and I would have missed out on what is my biggest blessing and learning.

"I am also very grateful over the last few years for the daytime care-givers who come into our home, Monday to Friday, to look after Hanif, who has grown increasingly attached to them. It has allowed me to take on part-time work as a hairdresser, to volunteer with children, and to attend congregational prayers daily, helping me achieve balance in my life."

Lessons

Life can sometimes deal unexpected cards. While many people might have chosen to give up caring for a severely developmentally challenged child, Nilofer was very clear about what she felt were the negative consequences of doing so. Therefore, she made many personal sacrifices over the years to achieve her goal of caring for Hanif at home, thus resulting in a very high quality of life for him.

A second key lesson is how we deal with unexpected events. We can see them as negative or we can see them as blessings. In Nilofer's case, what has given her strength is her firm belief that her training and experience with developmentally handicapped children were simply divinely inspired preparation for her primary role—to look after her son.

➲ Now, It's Your Turn

Define below or in the workbook you downloaded the consequences of *not* achieving your goal. Make these as emotive as possible:

1.	
2.	
3.	
4.	
5.	

.

Chapter 7:

What Are the Obstacles to Achieving Your Goal?

Difficulties are meant to rouse, not discourage. The human spirit is to grow strong by conflict.

—*William Ellery Channing*

L ife throws us many challenges, which we often view as obstacles that prevent us from getting to our goals. Instead, you may want to consider *embracing* these obstacles. For in them lies the solution to achieving your goals.

Why? Well, over thousands of years, as a species, man has learned to out-think obstacles and find solutions. This has been the primary reason for our survival as a species, and for the progress we have made. So if you define your obstacles carefully, you will find that your mind very quickly finds solutions, no matter the circumstances. It's a remarkable skill we all have.

Few people exemplify how numerous obstacles can be overcome in order to lead a happy life more than my friend Maria Castella, a massage therapist I have known for the past fifteen years while I struggled with back pain.

---

* The names and some details in this story have been changed to protect the family's privacy.

Maria's Story and Her Promise

"We left Chile in 1988 because my husband was being sought by the Pinochet regime for his role in bringing attention to the state's increasing human rights abuses, which he was beginning to see in greater numbers in his role as an emergency room physician. We knew we had to flee soon, despite the comfortable life we had and my own success as a psychologist, so we made arrangements to leave Chile and landed in Toronto in late 1988 as visitors.

"We applied for refugee status, and after a year and a half were successful. In the meantime, Raoul worked very hard, taking any job, sometimes two at a time, to support us. But Raoul was becoming increasingly despondent at not being able to work in his chosen profession, and relations between us became stormy. I needed to be with my young daughter Sandra at home and could also not get certified as a psychologist. But I was determined to make things work, because I did not feel the children would have a bright future if we were to return to Chile, as Raoul wished to do.

"Soon, we separated, and while Raoul continued to work in Toronto, he eventually decided to return to Chile since the political climate had improved. He wanted us to go back with him, and when I refused, saying the children were increasingly Canadian, their future lay in Canada, and it would be a very difficult adjustment for them, he got very angry, left the country, and promised never to support them. He has kept his word, despite being very successful, and he maintains no contact with our children.

"I knew in my heart, however, that I was making the right choice, and I began taking any job I could to support myself and my two growing children. I have cleaned homes, worked at retail jobs, and taught yoga. Each job I took, I did well, without any complaint, because I believe that who you are as an individual does not change when you take on different work. It is a value and perspective that I have instilled in my children.

"While I was keen in the initial years to get recertified as a psychologist, I was born dyslexic, so studying in Spanish, my native language, was difficult enough. I could never get a sufficient grasp of English, so I knew that it would be impossible for me to learn English well enough to pass my psychology exams.

"My focus for the children as they were growing up was to ensure that they had solid ethics and values and as broad an understanding of the world as possible. So I insisted on teaching Spanish to my son Jorge, in which he remains completely fluent today. Sandra can speak and understand Spanish, but her writing is of a lower quality.

"With the little I earned, I ensured I bought books for us each month; the children saw lots of theater performances, usually in the most dis-counted sections; they participated in ballet and jazz and learned to appre-ciate art; and they were active in various low-cost sports. I was determined that my limited financial resources were not going to be obstacles to my ambitions for my children.

"We would also travel for short vacations, camping in parks north of Toronto. I have a morbid fear of being attacked by bears, but I swallowed hard and just did it because I wanted to ensure my children appreciated nature, something they saw little of in our small one-bedroom apartment in a large high-rise building. As the kids grew older, around university age, I insisted they travel as much as possible. They had to be extremely frugal, as I had very little money, but they saved up money from summer jobs and tutoring other students. Travel they did, and it has helped shape them into the wonderful young adults they are today.

"I have no regrets about the sometimes very difficult years that I faced and the many obstacles in my path. I am blessed with two healthy, wonder-ful, well-adjusted children, and we live in a terrific country. I have many friends, and I love teaching yoga in addition to the few clients I still see as a massage therapist. And throughout these years, I have been blessed to be able to volunteer my time at a local South American cultural center, often with the elderly who long for company.

"As the kids get settled into their careers, I have begun working as a volunteer with disabled children. I am hopeful I can become a teacher's assistant and continue to help many young children with emotional and learning difficulties in the years ahead."

Lessons

Many times, Maria had the choice of going back to Chile to live a very comfortable life. Instead, she chose to single-handedly raise and support two young children in one of the most expensive cities in her newly adopted country. She did so despite her own language challenges, the inability to practice a profession for which she had trained and then worked hard at, and the inability to practice the excellent counseling skills she had developed, all without financial or other support from an increasingly successful ex-spouse. As a single mother, she was able to overcome her many obstacles because she was steadfast in her goal of bringing up her children to have the highest ethics and values.

Today, Jorge is in his late twenties and already a highly successful investment banker. Sandra is an A+ student and is soon beginning work at one of the most respected management consulting firms in Canada. They are wonderful, well-adjusted young adults, for what Maria could not give them because of financial obstacles, she more than made up for with love and care. Sacrifices she made and the non-negotiable insistence that they should both be well-educated made the difference, combined with a focus on the highest ethics and values. She ensured that no obstacle would get in the way of these goals.

➲ Now, It's Your Turn

List below or in the workbook you downloaded all the obstacles you can think of that may prevent you from reaching your goal, in as much detail as possible. Every time you do this, you will observe an amazing phenomenon. As you list your obstacles, your mind will move into problem-solving mode and start thinking immediately of solutions. Not all solutions will come at once. But over time, you can be confident that you will come up with solutions to every one of the obstacles you list, no matter how big an obstacle may initially seem. Just try it.

1.	
2.	
3.	
4.	
5.	
6.	
7.	
8.	
9.	
10.	

Having listed your obstacles, are you already thinking of solutions? Hold onto these thoughts for the next chapter.

Chapter 8:

What Are the Solutions to Overcoming Your Obstacles?

Every problem has a gift for you in its hands.

—Richard Bach

In the last chapter, you defined the obstacles to your goal. Now your mind will suddenly perceive solutions where none existed before. Why? I suggest that it's because, as a species, humans are instinctive problem-solvers. Furthermore, once obstacles are put down on paper, perspective changes. But if we don't put them down on paper, challenges usually loom large in our minds, where they keep growing and growing and growing.

The story of my friend Keith Rieger that follows illustrates how it's possible to overcome seemingly huge obstacles.

Keith's Story and His Promise

"One of my major life goals was to finish the Western States 100-Mile Running Race (www.WS100.com). This legendary race is held the last weekend in June every year and traverses the mountains of an old mining trail between Squaw Valley, California, and Auburn, California.

"I first discovered this race when I saw it on *ABC's Wide World of Sports* in the early 1980s. At the time, *Outside Magazine* named it 'The World's Toughest Race.'

"After learning this, I figured the WS100 would be the truest test of the running talents God had given me and might inspire my family, friends, and the Special Olympic athletes I coached to strive for their own significant goals. Therefore I set a goal to someday finish it.

"Easier said than done, right? Well, there were a few major obstacles along the way.

"First, I had to qualify. The WS100 requires you to qualify by finishing a sanctioned fifty-mile race within nine hours. Therefore I researched Web sites, magazines, and books, and I talked to other experienced ultramarathoners about the best way to prepare for and compete in an ultramarathon. Fortunately I prepared well both physically and mentally over a three-month period and finished the Mad Dog 50 Mile Road Race in Scottsdale, Arizona, with a time of 6:54:10.

"Second, I had to be chosen in a lottery. The WS100 limits each year's field to 435 participants (to comply with their U.S. Forest Service permit) by holding a lottery for the thousands of applicants. Therefore, I ensured my application was filled out correctly and sent in on time. Fortunately, I was picked for the 2006 event.

"Third, I had to train (a lot). The WS100 demands that you run for over fifteen hours, up and down significant mountains, and in 100°F+ temperatures. Therefore I developed a six-month training schedule and followed it closely. This included preparing for the long hours by building up my mileage to about one hundred miles per week, including a long run of about ten hours; preparing for the hills by doing a lot of runs on the treadmill with a 15 percent incline or a 7 percent decline (I was living in Florida at the time and had no hills in the vicinity); and preparing for the hot temperatures by running in the middle of the day (very hot and humid in May/June in Central Florida!).

"Finally, I had to complete the race. It was truly a challenge. The first four miles were straight up the Squaw Valley ski hill to an elevation of about 9,000 feet. The next ten miles were mostly through snow and streams of winter runoff water. Eventually, the trail made it to the lower elevations and sun-baked canyons, where the temperatures exceeded 105°F.

"Consequently, the dropout rate was almost 50 percent, and the winning time was two and a half hours slower than usual. Anticipating these challenges, I started conservatively and was careful to refuel as best as possible. However, at the thirty-mile check-in, I had lost six pounds and was in serious trouble, as were many of the participants around me. I slowed down for the next five miles and adjusted my salt intake. Shortly thereafter, I started feeling relatively better and was able to pick up my pace and maintain my weight.

"However, I still had a long way to go and many other potential obstacles to face. Many times throughout the race, doubt would creep into my thoughts and I would wonder how I would ever finish. Would I be able to maintain proper hydration, nutrition, electrolytes, etc.? Would my muscles, joints, and significant blisters be able to endure the pounding? Would I succumb to sleep deprivation or hypothermia late at night? Would I have equipment failure or get lost?

"To overcome these negative thoughts, I decided to break down my large goal of running the remaining sixty-five miles into a set of smaller goals—simply making it from aid station to aid station (spaced five miles apart). At each aid station, I would re-evaluate my condition and reset my goal of making it to the next aid station.

Fortunately, God saw me through each of these challenges and helped me achieve my ultimate goal of making it to the finish in a time of 26:27:33. In retrospect, I am amazed at what the human body can do and what the human mind can do when you take things one step at a time and determine to never give up, no matter the obstacles."

Here are some of Keith's favorite quotes associated with the WS100:

"The amazing thing about the Western States is that you show up at the starting line in the best shape of your life and a day later you show up at the finish line in the worst shape of your life."—Alan Black

"Running the Western States hurts for few days; however, if you quit, the ride from the aid station to the finish hurts all year."—Wayne Miles

"If you feel good running the Western States, don't worry. You'll get over it."—Gene Thibeault

"Western States does not test one's character, it reveals it."—Chris O'Brien

Lessons

Keith shows us how setting a huge goal, focusing on it, preparing well, and chunking up the goal into smaller, manageable pieces helped him complete the world's toughest race.

➲ Now, It's Your Turn

Rewrite your obstacles below or in the workbook you downloaded. Next to them, brainstorm one or more possible solutions. If you find that you are unable to define all the solutions on the first try, don't worry. Just keep coming back to this list, and eventually solutions will come to you. Remember, problem solving is ingrained in our nature.

	Obstacles	Solutions
1.		
2.		
3.		
4.		
5.		
6.		
7.		
8.		
9.		
10.		

This worksheet is contained within the free, downloadable workbook at www.KeepAnyPromise.com/workbook.

Chapter 9:

What Resources Can Help You Attain Your Goal?

Until one is committed, there is hesitancy, the chance to draw back. Concerning all acts of initiative (and creation), there is one elementary truth the ignorance of which kills countless ideas and splendid plans: that the moment one definitely commits oneself, then Providence moves too. All sorts of things occur to help one that would never otherwise have occurred. A whole stream of events issues from the decision, raising in one's favor all manner of unforeseen incidents and meetings and material assistance, which no man could have dreamed would have come his way. Whatever you can do, or dream you can do, begin it. Boldness has genius, power, and magic in it. Begin it now.

—Goethe

Often when facing a goal, we feel we have to accomplish the work on our own. Why do we put this pressure on ourselves? There are many, many resources in the universe that we can tap into. We need only ask. Since your ultimate aim is to achieve your goal, does it matter if you achieve your goal on your own, or if you get help along the way? Enlisting the help of those around you (and I am deeply convinced that most people *want* to help) makes it much easier to reach your destination. So enlist every resource you can in helping you achieve your goals.

In the spring of 2005, I was invited to speak to a small group of young entrepreneurs. Fresh from having climbed Mt. Kilimanjaro, I shared the lessons I learned from the climb as a metaphor for achieving any goal they set for themselves. The group thanked me warmly and presented me with a certificate indicating that they had donated a bedkit on my behalf. One more child in the developing world would soon sleep well.

I looked up the Web site for Sleeping Children Around the World (www.scaw.org), the bedkit sponsor, and was intrigued by the story of Murray Dryden and his wife Margaret. Since its establishment in 1970, this unique charity has raised more than $21 million and distributed bedkits to over 925,000 children in thirty-two developing countries. I am honored to share their story.

Murray's Story and His Promise

Murray was born on a farm in Domain, Manitoba, in 1911 and knew the meaning of hard work and a loving family. After leaving home during the Depression years, like many others, Murray found it difficult to find work. He became a door-to-door peddler, subsisting on what little cash he could earn. While traveling east through Canada, he slept in train stations many nights, after he rode the rails from one small town to another. He learned then what it was to be deprived of a good night's sleep.

During the 1950s in Toronto, Murray pursued a hobby in photography. One night he was particularly taken by the peaceful pose of his sleeping daughter, Judy, and took her photo. This led to photographing more and more children as they slept, in order to publish a coffee-table book.

One night while traveling in Pakistan, Murray tripped over a child sleeping on the street. A man of ideas, he decided that he must and would do something for children who did not have a suitable bed. He couldn't feed the world, but he believed a good night's sleep could make a hungry child's life more comfortable. Murray soon became a champion for children with often little or no hope for a future, in developing countries without welfare systems or medical insurance systems. Thus, with a strong desire to help others and a firm belief that with God nothing is impossible, in 1970, Sleeping Children Around the World began, initially distributing fifty bedkits in Pune, India.

What exactly is a bedkit? A bedkit recently distributed in Chennai, India, contained twenty-three items intended to provide each child with a safe and peaceful night's sleep. Bedkit items vary by country and include such things as a mattress, quilt, pillow, towels, mosquito net, shirt, shorts or dress, woolen blanket, plastic bucket, and school supplies. Recently, an insecticide-treated mosquito net has been included in malaria hot spots in Africa, where children are dying from malaria at the alarming rate of one every thirty seconds.

Murray and Margaret devoted their retirement to this program, initially hoping to raise $1 million. After this was achieved, they set a new goal of a million bedkits, which the organization hopes to reach by 2009 through the support of a growing legion of contributors.

Murray's initial goal was to raise $1 million. How did he get to $21 million? Simply by enlisting the help of thousands of donors, both to contribute towards the bedkits, each costing thirty-five dollars, and the help of volunteers, who pay their own way to deliver and oversee the distribution of the bedkits. He asked, the universe delivered. He took action, then he asked for more. The universe delivered more. Could he have accomplished what he did on his own? Most certainly not, and Murray was smart enough to know it.

What is remarkable is that 100 percent of all donations is used directly for the purchase of bedkits. All administrative expenses are covered by the interest from a trust fund bequeathed by the Drydens to the charity. And volunteers from Canada help distribute every shipment of bedkits, committing their time and resources to this wonderful cause.

Murray passed away in 2004. One of his favorite quotes was, "There is nothing more peaceful than a sleeping child."

Lessons

Murray vividly shows us how enlisting the assistance of others can help not only keep our own promises, but, as in his case, reach an even higher, previously unimaginable goal. Do you seek the help of others in order to attain your dreams?

➲ Now, It's Your Turn

Define below or in the workbook you downloaded the resources that you can enlist to help you achieve your goal. Resources can be people, tools, financial or spiritual systems, or anything you wish. You might also want to include the resources that you would like to enlist, but feel you cannot for one reason or another.

Revisit the list a few times: you will be surprised at how your list grows. Then look carefully at those resources that you didn't think you could enlist, and think harder, talk to others, and let your mind ponder this seeming impossibility. Watch what happens!

1.	
2.	
3.	
4.	
5.	
6.	
7.	
8.	
9.	
10.	

When you get an opportunity to contribute to someone else's huge goal or dream, go out of your way to help others achieve their goals. What goes around, comes around.

Chapter 10:

What Are Your Ninety-Day Milestones?

Don't say you don't have enough time. You have exactly the same number of hours per day that were given to Helen Keller, Pasteur, Michaelangelo, Mother Teresa, Leonardo de Vinci, Thomas Jefferson, and Albert Einstein.

—H. Jackson Brown

Sometimes reaching a goal feels miraculous, like a quantum leap. But if you look closely, you'll notice that the goal was attained by moving from one step to the next. To make steady progress, it is critical to define steps and timeframes along the way. Timeframes allow you to assess your goal, determine your progress, and take corrective action. Well-defined steps with clear timeframes are often referred to as milestones.

Speaking of milestones reminds me of my friend Lisa Rowles. I first met her after a particularly intense day at *Life Mastery,* a one-week workshop run by the Tony Robbins Company in Palm Springs, California in October 2005. Over many talks and walks, my wife and I got to know her well, and we could see that Lisa was extremely stressed. Though she was younger than us by a few years, she looked older.

Lisa's Story and Her Promise

"When I met Karim and Narmin at *Life Mastery* in Palm Springs in October 2005, I was at a crossroads in my life. I don't think I realized this as consciously as it seems now, but I had just come out of an addictive and abusive relationship, was treading water professionally, and feeling like I should be happy with my lot but was somehow missing a big piece of the puzzle.

"On the face of it, I was a successful, self-supporting single girl with my own home and a good social life. Beneath the exterior, I wondered what life had in store for me. Was this it? I was holding out for a better relationship, but starting to wonder if this was realistic. Could I truly expect to meet a worthy partner who kept me on my toes and yet supported me, without expectations, with his own dreams that would mingle with mine?

"Professionally, I felt the need to prove to myself that I could step off the corporate ladder and follow a different path, yet I was terrified of the potential financial instability that could ensue. In this inner turmoil, enjoying autumn Californian sun, I was instantly struck by Karim and Narmin's honesty and generosity, and by Karim's calm and peaceful energy.

"At that time, I could not have foreseen the changes that were about to occur in my life. This in itself is strange, as I'd already made some significant changes up to this point (changing career paths, living in different countries, divorce, to name a few). This inability to recognize my own potential had shown up regularly in my life and was one of the many reasons I chose to pursue coaching as a profession.

"*Life Mastery* enabled me to take stock of my life, personally, financially, spiritually, physically, and mentally. I met many wonderful people, all of whom came together to learn and grow, and I learned that being vulnerable and honest with myself about my own misgivings, fears, and concerns and voicing them to others helped move me forward.

"Returning from Palm Springs, whilst equipped to manage far better on a number of levels, I didn't have the same level of support mechanism back home. I spent time mapping my vision and my goals, and started taking care of myself more effectively mentally, physically, and spiritually. I spent time 'being' instead of constantly 'doing.' I started listening to the voice within—noticing my instincts and being brave enough to follow them. I also set ninety-day milestones for what I wanted to achieve, even though sometimes I had no idea how I would go about achieving these milestones; other times, the milestones were hazy.

"In the months that followed, I meditated daily on my connection with the wider world, noticing every opportunity, every coincidence. Going inside myself, I went back to early childhood dreams and reconnected with what had seemed impossible.

"One of these dreams was formed as a five-year-old, as I held what was clearly a sad and drugged-up lion cub at a circus. Despite the dreadful circumstances, my innocent child's brain told me this is what I want to do when I grow up—I would feed lion cubs and free them into the wild (this was in the era of Joy and George Adamson and Elsa the lioness of *Born Free* fame—highly evocative for a young cat-lover). Amazingly, in my attempt at growing up, I'd lost touch with that childhood dream, and now suddenly it stood in front of me. Within twenty-four hours of having the thought, I googled 'walking with lions' and immediately found Antelope Park, in Zimbabwe. Despite having a very busy full-time job, I knew that come what may, I needed to make this trip and take the month out to be a volunteer at Antelope Park.

"Somehow, despite the seeming impossibility, I made a case for going, listed the pros and cons, prepared answers for all the 'no go' areas, and, most importantly, got into the best, most positive, powerful, and focused state of mind possible to have the conversation with my managing director. Bingo! Within weeks it was booked, and I was going.

"Actually, making the booking and knowing I intended to do this, even if it meant losing my job, and that somehow it would work out, was new for me. I felt as if I was connecting with something much more powerful in my being, something that had been dormant for some time. As soon as

I made this commitment, everything in my life started to change. It was as though some unknown force (whether this is universal or within my own consciousness, who knows) took this as a sign that I truly intended to step up and was ready to make changes in my life.

"Within a month of booking the trip, I went on a four-day business conference on a cruise ship, as a career coach. It's fair to say that my energy was totally different at this point. I felt completely connected to the world, aware of my calling, knowing I was walking the right path at this stage of my life.

"The evening of day one of this trip, I was seated at dinner with a man representing a potential new client from the finance sector (a totally random seating: Roger and I might never have met if someone had changed the seating plan). We got on so well, I agreed to run a coaching session with him the following day, and we continued to talk daily at the conference.

"Roger supported me in preparing for my trip to Zimbabwe. And the experience there was totally awesome. I worked alongside volunteers and lion-handlers from six in the morning until six at night, feeding cubs, walking them, making fences, snare-sweeping. Being around fourteen cubs, varying in age from six weeks to twenty-two months (and 100kg!) was the most amazing experience.

"Instinctively, I know that somewhere down the line, big cats will feature more prominently in my life. I'm just not sure how and when yet, so I'm allowing my instinct to provide the pathway to enable me to realize how this will unfold, and to be ready when it does.

"Roger and I have now been together for eighteen months. One of the things that stood out in Roger's mind was the fact that I had taken the plunge to follow my 'calling' and my instincts in going to Zimbabwe to walk with lions. He was and is in total support of my intention to continue to be a volunteer with big cats on an annual or every-eighteen-month basis.

"The coincidences and opportunities have just snowballed from here. Being with Roger gave me the confidence to step out and become a free-lance business coach and consultant, which I have successfully done for twelve months. I've gone from being single and corporately employed to partnered, with two dogs, a new home, and a freelance consultancy.

"The latest *piece de resistance* occurred in June 2007. When I met Roger, he had a dream to climb Mont Blanc (at 4810m, the largest mountain peak in Europe) for charity, with the support and involvement of his employers, St James's Place. For me, Mont Blanc represented some of my greatest dislikes and fears: extreme cold, exposure, fatigue, and prolonged endurance. For all of these reasons, I decided that this would be the ultimate challenge: stepping up to live a dream is one thing, stepping up to challenge huge fears is another!

"As a result of our meeting on that ship, Roger put his case forward, using all the tools and techniques at his disposal, and six months later, we returned from Mont Blanc. Fifteen of us made it to the final 300 meters. Twelve of us, including me, made the summit; the others were air-lifted due to injury.

"Our guides were some of the best and most experienced in the business. Without them, we would have failed. Mont Blanc is the hardest thing I've ever done. None of us were truly prepared for the weather conditions (unexpected blizzards and high winds), the lack of sleep (just four hours in thirty-six), the vertical climbs on rock and snow for 800 meters, and the severe effect altitude has on the ability to breathe above 4,000 meters (15,000 feet).

"How did we do it? The same way we all achieve anything. Have a dream, vividly visualize yourself completing that dream (make pictures of it that you display somewhere you see regularly, such as posters on walls, screensavers, etc.), voice it openly and realistically, plan your daily activity, and believe you can do it. Determination, focus, and expert assistance are the final jewels in your goal-setting crown.

"I won't climb Mont Blanc again (my boots went on eBay as soon as I returned), but I will put other challenges in place, to remind me of my ability to overcome my own boundaries, step out of my comfort zone, and to be open to new and exciting possibilities.

"Roger now has his big dream in place—Everest in 2009. And I'm in the process of deciding what my next trip will be, having spent part of May 2008 caring for cheetahs at a wildlife sanctuary in Namibia. It's likely to be Africa and involve more big cats.

"I know that my purpose is to serve others and, in so doing, to learn about myself and my capacity to learn and grow. We all have that knowing inside, it's just a question of accessing the signals, putting a plan in place, and keeping focused on the milestones along the way."

Lessons

Lisa's story dramatically illustrates how very realistic it is to completely turn around one's life. She shows us how planning carefully, visualizing the results, taking action, and setting milestones along the way is vital to achieving our dreams. Who could have imagined such a transformation in so short a time?

➲ Now, It's Your Turn

Repeat below or in the workbook you downloaded the *huge* goal you listed in Chapter 1 in the left column. Confirm how you will measure achievement of your goal in the middle column. Now, define your milestones, i.e., where could you be in the next ninety days? Be as specific as you can about your milestones in order to easily measure them. Later, you will have the opportunity to create milestones for future ninety-day periods and all your goals.

Goal (from Chapter 1)	How you will measure it (from Chapter 3)	Milestones for the next 90 days
		1
		2
		3
		4
		5

Chapter 11:

With Whom Will You Share This Goal?

In my experience, there is only one motivation, and that is desire. No reasons or principle can contain it or stand against it.

—*Jane Smiley*

Sharing your goal with others is vital to your success. You might feel uncomfortable at first, but hiding your goal will not help you. Instead, you will find that when you have the courage to share your goal, you articulate it more clearly for yourself, and you strengthen your commitment to your goal. Sharing your goal also allows you to receive objective feedback; by sharing your *huge* goal, you will undoubtedly inspire friends, family, and colleagues. So please consider doing what we always ask children to do, and share!

During the hike up Mt. Kilimanjaro in January 2005, I was fortunate to have Paulo Laizer as a guide. Paulo was a Maasai who had left his traditional homeland to work as a mountain guide. But he wanted to be able to contribute actively to the development of his village. He shared this goal with an Australian, Donna Duggan, who was moving permanently to Arusha, Kilimanjaro—climb headquarters. Paulo had met Donna on a previous climb. Together with Naseeb Ismail, a Tanzanian, the three of them began a company called Maasai Wanderings, in order to both provide a great travel experience to visitors and help in the development of Paulo's village. I subsequently got to know Donna when she stepped in at the eleventh hour to help organize a trip for high school students that had run into organizational difficulty.

Donna's Story and Her Promise

"I was born in Brisbane, Australia. I had one older brother and very hard-working parents. I grew up helping my parents in the fresh produce businesses that they owned from as far back as I can remember.

"After secondary school, I got itchy feet after a few family trips abroad, and at nineteen, I headed off to the UK to work as a nanny. After two years, I packed my bag and spent the next six months wandering around Europe, mostly by myself or with other lone female travelers for company. I loved the freedom, the challenge, and learning about the varying cultures.

"I then went back to the UK and met up with my friend and we had the audacious idea of trying to walk from Cape Town to Cairo, so off we went. We clambered aboard post trucks, on the backs of bicycles, dhows, and various other ludicrous contraptions and eventually made it in one piece to Somalia from Cape Town, after about two months.

"As we were sitting one evening in Somalia planning our next move, we looked at each other and declared that we missed Tanzanian hospitality, openness, and caring. So we headed south again and stayed there a couple of months, wandering north to south and east to west. We loved Tanzania and all it had to offer.

"We went home, and all I found was a burning desire to return to Africa. So I convinced another friend to walk from Cape Town to Cairo with me—she was ready after all my adventure stories from the previous trip—and off we went. Once again, but this time on a dhow on the Somali/Kenya border, we looked at each other and decided that Tanzania was calling. Back we went, wandering around, enjoying the Tanzanian lifestyle and its trials and tribulations.

"I did it a third year in a row as well. Each time I went back to Tanzania, I learned more and more about the people and the cultures, and the dreams and needs of many. And each time that I left Tanzania, I left a little piece of me behind. So I disappeared home and spent the next few years studying for my nursing degree. I knew the best way for me to help with impact was to have vital skills that would allow me to make a difference. After I graduated, off I wandered, back and forth. I would spend months at home in Brisbane doing all sorts of crazy fundraising ventures—wine dinners, cake stalls, moustache shavings, walkathons—until I had gathered enough funds to send vaccines, syringes, and other general medical equipment to Tanzania, where I would be waiting for it, to spend the following one or two months jabbing away, weighing babies, offering education classes, etc.

"After a while of doing this, I felt that I wasn't achieving enough, and the lines of the helpless were growing longer. So in 2004, after meeting my husband Naseeb, we decided on a different tactic. We decided that because he was a safari guide and I was a bit of a 'helper,' we would combine our two passions and create something where we could use all of our skills on one project and try and make a more meaningful difference through education. This is not saying that nobody should receive medical help if they needed it, but after seeing the typical patient (young, uneducated) come through day after day, we decided that perhaps 'young and uneducated' could turn into just young!

"Therefore, in September 2004, Maasai Wanderings was born. The name Maasai Wanderings comes from our desire to help the Maasai people wherever we could, and also from the wandering of the recently circumscribed young Maasai warrior, or *morani*. After all, wandering is a trait both Naseeb and I shared prior to deciding we wanted to do something together!

"On July 11, 2005, we finally had saved enough money to start our nursery school in Ilkurot (a Maa word meaning 'dusty place'). We began with one teacher, forty-five students, and one old, disused classroom. For the next six months, we continued to take as many people as we could on safari, up Kilimanjaro, and on other adventures in the hope that we could raise enough funds to start building our own classroom at least. We also began sharing our goals with anyone who cared to listen, and people were very supportive and generous. Some contributed funds, others pitched in to help at the school, yet others sent supplies. Some even offered to return to help with the school on a longer-term basis.

"On January 9, 2006, we opened Ilkurot Nursery School, which consisted of a classroom, desks, pencils, a teacher, and daily porridge. And not long after: six toilets, storage cupboards, a kitchen complete with stove (firewood), store, staff room, and sick-bay. We had also managed two water tanks—one for trying to get some water to the areas surrounding the classrooms (as the dust was irritating the eyes of the students and conjunctivitis was rampant), and one plumbed into the kitchen. As of January 2007, we had an intake of 212 nursery school students, with all aspects of their education at this level supplied to them, down to their uniforms and exercise books. By June 2008, we had grown to serve 1,652 students, from nursery school to the end of primary school, plus secondary sponsorships for 29 students from Ilkorut Primary School.

"Although continuing to focus on the nursery school, we are looking next door to the primary school a little more. We constructed more classrooms and refurbished the oldest mud brick classrooms. We have also supplied thousands of textbooks—there were none before—and have also presented the teaching staff with a manual typewriter (more on the way) and a duplicating machine.

"In the future, I would like to sponsor more teachers to assist in the school and for the current teachers to undergo continual assessment and training. I would like to build another nursery school building because there are still more young children wanting to enter our classroom, but we are bursting at the seams. I would like to see many, many more books available to the children for their studies, perhaps a library.

"I have encountered many speed bumps along the way: losing containers of supplies to corruption, theft of personal and educational items, fraud, the bureaucracy of the Maasai elderdom, building deadlines, etc., but I feel essentially all of this doesn't really matter because we *are* getting somewhere and we *are* making a difference.

"It still amazes me, the thirst that these kids have for knowledge. I dream that with the right resources, the right attitude, and the right support, we could see a president emerge from this village: someone who has struggled against all odds to pass the finish line and understands the need for grass-roots assistance throughout Tanzania.

"By sharing all my ideas with my husband and my family and friends, I have gained the most amazing support network, from previous clients to friends of friends. Each person wanting to support me, trusting in me, and knowing that my love for this project will always help me make the right decisions for the benefit of others, has spurred me along.

"A friend of mine once said: 'Donna, there are people like you and there are people like me: we can't do each other's work but we can't do without each other.' And I believe it is true: the support of those around you is paramount to any successful goal or dream, but this can only come about if you first share your huge promises."

Lessons

Donna's story shows us how sharing her dreams has helped her jump-start her goal. In fact, through one of the climbs Narmin and I organized, a teacher volunteered to spend a year at the school. She is working closely with Donna to set up a long-term support system to fuel Donna's dreams even further.

➲ Now, It's Your Turn

You will find it most helpful if you share your goal with people who will give you encouragement and feedback. They should also challenge you when you are having difficulty. Be careful, though, of naysayers (and there are plenty of them), for they will undermine your confidence. So select this small group carefully, and keep them updated regularly, for they will spur your progress.

List below or in the workbook you downloaded at least three people with whom you would like to share your goals and who you will commit to updating regularly, ideally every two weeks.

1.	
2.	
3.	
4.	
5.	

You are almost there. The next step is really the icing on the cake, but a vital final step in helping you keep any promise you choose to make.

Chapter 12:

What Will Your Goal Look Like, Feel Like, and Sound Like?

The future belongs to people who see possibilities before they become obvious.

—*Ted Levitt*

No Olympic athlete or world-class performer ever achieved success without imagining him or herself as a champion, standing on the podium. You will find that visualizing success as vividly as you can (use photos, mental images, detailed descriptions to show you what it will *feel* like) is a vital step to achieving and exceeding your biggest goals.

Gail Nielsen from London, Ontario, the executive coach I was blessed to work with (www.extraordinarymoves.com), used similar visualization principles to help me see vividly how it would feel for this book to be a tremendous success. I could imagine the book helping hundreds of thousands of people achieve huge goals in their lives and then myself receiving regular feedback on such accomplishments. My visualization spurred me to start and complete the book in record time, given my already full schedule. This vision also sustained me when I encountered many obstacles along the way.

Gail's Story and Her Promise

"If I trace back, in years, my experience of trying to make my desires manifest, I find myself in the summer of 1997. I was in my mid-twenties, working on my Master's thesis, my husband fresh out of school and looking for employment. I had always been ambitious and knew that I could do great and meaningful work in my life. But how was it all to play out? I was on the verge of taking what I was determined would be a single year off from academia after my Master's, to make some money before beginning my doctoral work.

"Well, here I am, doctorate-free ten years later, and I am so grateful for the way the journey has unfolded.

"I can picture myself during that summer sitting on the porch of our house in London, Ontario, reading a book that my husband had bought at a garage sale, ironically. It's a little book of about a hundred pages, but one that set the stage, in a way, for the life I'm living now—a life of certain contentment, abundance, and joy I really never knew were possible. It was Deepak Chopra's *Creating Affluence—Wealth Consciousness in the Field of All Possibilities.* I first read the principles then and they absolutely worked to the degree that I employed them. But I didn't really start 'working the program' until …

"Fast forward six years. Before the transformation I'm about to describe, I had been brimming with the potential for greatness, but I wasn't challenging myself to own it and step into it. I was holding myself back in major ways. All of my adult life, I had longed to become an author and professional speaker and to be in a position from which I could assist others in living their most fulfilling and meaningful lives. I had some sense that I had the natural gifts to do these things. But the white noise of the life I had created was making inaudible the messages that would lead me down this path directly. For years, I neglected these callings, and I found it difficult to tend whatever seeds I did plant because in many ways, and as many people are, I was locked into the box of my own limiting beliefs.

"For example, I had started writing several books and articles to no avail; I had stints of consulting, teaching, and conducting presentations, but I just didn't believe I was in the zone; I had myself convinced that bursting through financial ceilings was hard work. I had made some great strides as a singer/songwriter, but just wasn't breaking through and producing that ground-breaking CD, and my private practice in counseling just wasn't doing it for me.

"Given all the things that seemed to be going right in my life during all those years in between, which were in fact right enough in their own way, it was difficult to identify how scarily off track my life was actually veering. Underneath the surface I was deeply frustrated and my heart was becoming increasingly closed. I was angry and confused, unsure of how to proceed. It was lonely territory—nobody seemed to understand what I was going through—and I felt pulled in a hundred different directions.

"It took a long series of dark and painful life experiences over several years, including the death of my father, bitter fallings-out with loved ones, emotional exhaustion, and culminating with a near-miss accident that could have taken my life, to plunge me into my dark night of the soul—the wakeup call I desperately needed to start creating my real life once and for all.

"From the terrifying climax of the near-miss, I was forced to face myself on every level. After the event, tremendous amounts of crude and almost incapacitating fear seemed to let loose within and all around me. I had no choice but to make the journey, which took many, many months, through that fear to find new ways of navigating life. The key was in developing the will to envision what was possible for a better life, to be able to entertain a place of light and possibility while still treading water in utter darkness. Yet, I did it; step by focused step, daily meditation after daily meditation, developing the capacity to hold my own, until—at last and in the early light of day—I reached dry land.

"This painful 'dark night' experience—which I used to try desperately to make disappear—I know now has been my supreme gift. As a result of generating the strength to work with it creatively, my life is now brimming, from a balanced center, with hope, authentic power, opportunities, riches of all kinds, and a depth of feeling that I could simply not experience when I was trying to force my expansive, possibility-filled life into a tiny, supposedly safe compartment.

"I practice gratitude as a daily way of life now. My inner entrepreneur and my inner academic have become friends, and I'm no longer afraid of stuff that used to knock me off my feet. I choose love and compassion, instead of small-mindedness and judgment, as my reference points for everything.

"Now the work I do every day in my coaching and writing focuses on helping others become open to radically vast potential that may make no sense from their current limited perspective. Is it not our greatest opportunity *and* responsibility to haul out courage enough to see and taste what's good and true, but seems almost inconceivably out of reach? My take on it now is that we absolutely need to do it; *the world needs us to do it.*

"As I have grown more honest, creative, and daring enough to articulate my goals—now here's the key—with a radical commitment to *trust* that good things are intended for me, the door of possibility has swung wide open. I'm truly grateful to those in the world who have beheld, for the rest of us, the notion that tremendous things are in fact possible for ourselves and the planet if we develop ourselves in the right way. And so I continue to embrace the opportunity to develop a stronger capacity to look beyond my current circumstances, whatever they might be, and to listen to and feel each desire as if it is *already* gifted to me. It unfailingly shows up in one form or another, often better than I had imagined, and usually with a twist—the universe's clever way of keeping me humble."

Lessons

Gail's story shows us how important is it to make the effort to visualize, hear, and feel what you are seeking, as clearly you can. By keeping her eye on this vision of her future, no matter the circumstances of her life, she was able to emerge out of darkness into a wonderful new life that leaves her completely fulfilled and makes a growing impact on the world. And on a very personal note, had Gail not helped me visualize this book and its possibilities, I would never have written it!

➲ Now, It's Your Turn

Use the space below or in the workbook you downloaded to visualize your goal when it is achieved at the end of the timeframe you defined in Chapter 2. Be as descriptive as possible, using words, photographs, and sketches.

_____

_____

_____

_____

_____

_____

_____

_____

_____

_____

See, It Was Easy!

> *Without goals, and plans to reach them, you are like a ship that has set sail with no destination.*
>
> —*Fitzhugh Dodson*

Now that you have had the courage and taken the time to answer the questions posed in Chapters 1 to 12, I invite you to bring all these thoughts together and list them in one place.

1. Your most important and most *audacious* goal is: (make the goal inspiring and awesome, one that makes anyone reading it go wide-eyed!)

   _____

   _____

   _____

   _____

2. Your timeframe is:

   _____

   _____

   _____

   _____

3. You will measure achievement of your goal by:

   _____

   _____

   _____

   _____

4. Your compelling reasons for reaching your goal are:

_____

_____

_____

_____

5. The benefits/results you expect to get are:

_____

_____

_____

_____

6. The consequences of *not* achieving your goal are:

_____

_____

_____

_____

7. The obstacles to your achieving this goal are:

_____

_____

_____

_____

8. The solutions to overcoming the obstacles are:

_____

_____

_____

_____

9. The resources to help you attain your goal are:

_____

_____

_____

_____

10. Your ninety-day milestones are:

_____

_____

_____

_____

11. You will share this goal and information with:

_____

_____

_____

_____

12. Your goal will look like, feel like, sound like:

_____

_____

_____

_____

If you completed this exercise fully, you are on your way to becoming a powerful goal-setter. Remember: you can use these twelve steps to achieve *any* goal in the shortest possible time, with the least amount of strain.

For all your goals, make copies of the following blank worksheet, and think through the twelve steps carefully for each of your promises. As you complete your thinking in this systematic manner, you will find that you are already along the way to achieving your goals. This worksheet is also contained within the free, downloadable workbook at www.KeepAnyPromise.com/workbook.

Achieve *Any* Goal: Extra worksheet

Below is an extra worksheet that you can use to think through another goal. Practice makes perfect, so go through the same process for every goal.

1. Your most important and most *audacious* goal is: (make the goal inspiring and awesome, one that makes anyone reading it go wide-eyed!)

    _____

    _____

    _____

    _____

2. Your timeframe is:

    _____

    _____

    _____

    _____

3. You will measure achievement of your goal by:

    _____

    _____

    _____

    _____

4. Your compelling reasons for reaching your goal are:

    _____

    _____

    _____

    _____

5. The benefits/results you expect to get are:

_____

_____

_____

_____

6. The consequences of *not* achieving your goal are:

_____

_____

_____

_____

7. The obstacles to your achieving this goal are:

_____

_____

_____

_____

8. The solutions to overcoming the obstacles are:

_____

_____

_____

_____

9. The resources to help you attain your goal are:

_____

_____

_____

_____

10. Your ninety-day milestones are:

_____

_____

_____

_____

11. You will share this goal and information with:

_____

_____

_____

_____

12. Your goal will look like, feel like, sound like:

_____

_____

_____

_____

This worksheet is contained within the free, downloadable workbook at www.KeepAnyPromise.com/workbook.

Chapter 13:

The Spillover Effect

The difference between the impossible and the possible lies in a person's determination.

—*Tommy Lasorda*

Quite often, we have difficulty achieving our goals because they seem overwhelming and there are so many of them. What I learned was that as I made progress in one area, I started making progress in other areas. I termed this the spillover effect. I attribute this effect to four things:

1. The act of making progress in one area builds your confidence, and greater confidence makes goals in other areas look less daunting. Your increased confidence helps you take on more challenges.

2. The fear of failure that holds so many of us back from trying new things, from venturing too far from our comfort zones, gradually begins to diminish.

3. As you share your goals with the world, you start attracting the resources you need to achieve these goals. This is especially true of the goals based on helping others, making the world a better place, and having a positive impact in the world.

4. As you align more closely with your purpose in life, clarity and focus
   arrive, as well as a measured sense of calm that allows you to achieve
   more—quicker, faster, and easier.

I have outlined below a personal story that I believe perfectly illustrates
this principle.

Four years ago, in 2004, I had not sung publicly since I was twelve years
old. Yet I longed to participate in congregational singing, and in my heart,
I knew I could sing. One day, having made progress in many other areas in
my life, I made up my mind to find an expert who could coach me and who
would also give me honest feedback if, after listening to me, she thought
I was a terrible, tone-deaf singer.

We picked two devotional recitations whose tunes I liked (I later learned
that these were actually quite difficult recitations, but my coach never let
that interfere). A few weeks later, I recited these in front of a very small
audience during early morning prayer. Slowly, I began to overcome my
morbid fear of singing and thought if I could learn and sing fifty recitations (up from the fifteen or so I had learned as a child), I would be
extremely happy.

In 2005, my grandmother, then eighty-four years old, was slowly dying
of lung cancer, even though she had never been a smoker in her life (my
grandfather, long deceased, had). Whenever I was able to visit her, I would
sing a new recitation I had just learned. In the early days of her terminal
nine-month illness, she was able to join me in singing, and we formed a
deep bond as she related how she used to sing as a child.

I knew nothing about her childhood, though she was very close to me
as I was her first grandson. She had provided after-school care for me as a
child for many years while I was growing up in Kenya. Her stories of her
life as a young girl, newly emigrated to East Africa from India, were fasci-
nating. Getting to know her in this way was an unexpected spillover result
of my goal to learn fifty recitations.

When she could not sing anymore because she was too weak, she would simply hear me sing and gently acknowledge my singing.

One day, I proudly told her that I had learned twenty-five recitations and, even more proudly, that I planned to learn twenty-five more, for a grand total of fifty recitations learned and sung in congregation. She was extremely weak at this stage, having withered down to skin and bone, but still very alert mentally. She whispered to me, "Learn one hundred." I gulped, pretended I had not heard, and repeated my desire to learn fifty recitations. She raised her voice the tiniest bit, slowly turned to look straight at me, and in a clearer, audible whisper, repeated "Learn one hundred, dear." I knew she had got the better of me, and I committed to learning one hundred recitations. She passed away just a few weeks later.

In two years, I went on to learn and publicly sing one hundred recitations, some of them very complicated and rarely sung. I've obtained professional classical Indian music vocal training, sung repeatedly before hundreds, occasionally thousands, of people, and cut a CD of recitations. I am working on creating a set of CDs, with my singing coaches and other great singers I have come to know. I have also deepened my own spirituality, as the recitations are devotional in nature. Increasingly, I can understand their meanings, although they are composed mainly in Khojki, a language no longer spoken. I am hopeful that the CD set will bring love and joy to all listeners.

So, besides the many direct impacts arising from the singing listed above, what is the spillover impact?

I was so afraid of singing; having now repeatedly conquered this fear, I continue to conquer other fears with ease: public speaking, fundraising, climbing mountains, and, above all, writing this book.

I am convinced that had I not developed the willingness to occasionally make a mistake and to be judged every time I sing (because each congregation has many discerning and excellent singers), I would never have had the courage to undertake writing this book. The four benefits I outlined above—developing confidence, overcoming fear of failure,

attracting resources when we share goals, and alignment with one's purpose—are clearly illustrated by the spillover results that have come about
from my singing, which helped me overcome the many doubts I had before
starting to write this book.

Like most things in life, there is also a flip side to the spillover effect. For
example, if you recoil in fear at some things in life, you may find yourself carrying that behavior into other parts of your life. If you have a spillover pattern
based on fear and negativity versus confidence and achievement, even subconsciously, imagine how much harder you've been making your own life.

➲ Now, It's Your Turn

Think of an area of your life where you have made significant progress.
Did it have a spillover effect? How do you recognize it? Was it a positive
spillover or a negative one? How did the spillover show up in your life?
When was it most apparent? How did you respond to it? How could you
use this new knowledge to help you keep more promises in your life? Write
your thoughts below or in the workbook.

_____

_____

_____

_____

_____

I hope that from this chapter, you see that when you make significant progress in any area of your life, you almost always benefit from a spillover
effect. And likewise, when there is negative spillover, you need to keep that
in check so as to minimize impact on other areas of your life.

Chapter 14:

Strategic By-Products™

The pessimist sees difficulty in every opportunity. The optimist sees the opportunity in every difficulty.

—*Winston Churchill*

When we set huge goals, especially ones beyond our current capabilities, we often create unintended, unpredictable, and sometimes more valuable results. These results come from new knowledge (discoveries), new opportunities (surprises), and new capabilities (innovations) required to attain our goal. Discoveries, surprises, and innovations can sometimes be much more valuable than the original goal. And the more powerful the goal, the greater the possibility of such valuable strategic by-products.*

To illustrate with a personal example: five years ago, after beginning to recover from over two decades of back problems and a very debilitating three-month period of immobilization, and narrowly avoiding major back surgery, I decided to participate in a sixty-kilometer charity walk. To provide context: I could barely walk to the end of my driveway just a year prior to this decision. My goal: use the required training to improve my health and fitness levels, while raising funds for an important cause.

Four years later, I have completed four charity walks, recruited twenty people to walk as part of a team, fundraised much more than I could ever have imagined, spread awareness of breast cancer, and helped many in the group improve their health significantly. But something interesting—and completely unintended—happened along the way.

A fellow walker inspired me to climb Mt. Kilimanjaro, something he had just completed as a charity climb, raising over $100,000 for the Alzheimer's Society. My mind could not fathom the idea of either undertaking the climb or raising this amount of money. A year and a half after the inspiration, I climbed Kilimanjaro with my daughter. The next year, a climb we organized raised $50,000 for the Stephen Lewis Foundation; in 2007, three climbs raised $200,000 towards child education programs in Kenya and Tanzania. More climbs are being planned for Nepal, Peru, and Tanzania.

And my health? I have never felt fitter or healthier.

PART 2:

How Do I Implement My Goals and Stay Focused?

You were born to be a winner, but to be a winner you must plan to win and prepare to win.

—*Zig Zaglar*

You've worked hard to understand the essential steps to achieving any goal. It's now time to focus on implementation.

The next few chapters are key to the changes you may be thinking about making in your life, so take them to heart, and, bit by bit, use the simple techniques to begin a lifelong implementation, review, and reflection process. You will be amazed at how easy and, for many people, how natural this process can become after the first year.

Here we go ...

Chapter 15:

Where Do You Want to Be in *One Year* with Each of Your Goals?

> *There are no secrets to success. It is the result of preparation, hard work, and learning from failure.*
>
> —*Colin Powell*

Many people set annual goals, perhaps New Year's, birthday, or anniversary resolutions, or goals and objectives for work planning and budgeting. Do you? If so, do you find yourself generally achieving most of these goals, or not? If you want to keep your annual promises, then complete the section below. I have provided an example to guide you.

Timeframe: <u>Aug. 24, 2007 to Aug. 24, 2008 (my daughter's birthday)</u>

	Life Category	Where I am today (Aug. 2007)	My goals for the next 12 months
1	Write a bestseller so I can eventually help 5 million people achieve huge goals in their lives	· The bestseller draft is completed · Endorsements are in progress · Arrangements with publisher are in place	· Publish the book, and market it so that it reaches out to as many people as possible (100,000 in Year 1) · Launch the new Web site and have 10,000 subscribers by end of Year 1
2	Fitness	Hiked high in the Andes successfully with my daughter	Climb to Everest Base Camp

➲ Now, It's Your Turn

Complete this exercise, ideally on the worksheet you downloaded from www.KeepAnyPromise.com/workbook.

Timeframe: Year ending _____

	Life categories	Where I am today	My goals for the next 12 months
1			
2			
3			
4			
5			
6			
7			
8			
9			

I am certain that if you follow the twelve-step process outlined in Part 1, you will make great progress in the next twelve months toward achieving these goals.

➲ Don't Forget This Key Step

At the end of each year, I block off time in my next year's calendar for all those items that are particularly important to me. This is a key step in achieving my goals. I schedule time off; time to exercise; time with family, including dinners and birthdays; time for prayer, meditation, and high holidays; time for daily, weekly, monthly, ninety-day, and annual planning; time for board and committee meetings; and time for anything else that I deem especially important to me. Therefore, the remaining time is available for work and other important activities, but not at the expense of the most significant things in my life. As long as I stick to this schedule reasonably (and I generally tend to do so), I am in balance. The moment I start cancelling important prescheduled "appointments," I know I am losing balance.

I use Microsoft Outlook to do this, as it allows me to schedule recurring items easily. Whether you use a fancy software program or handwrite events into a diary does not matter. The key is to first schedule the most important things in your life in your calendar, and then let the rest be taken up with work and other commitments. Try it: I have used this system very successfully for the last three years.

As you do so, you will find that many of the time slots that you have blocked off are very directly related to the goals you just defined. As for other goals that you may not have included in your schedule, don't worry—you will have the opportunity to do just that in Chapter 17.

Chapter 16:

What Do You Plan to Achieve in the Next Ninety Days?

> *Inaction breeds doubt and fear. Action breeds confidence and courage. If you want to conquer fear, do not sit home and think about it. Go out and get busy.*
>
> —*Dale Carnegie*

In many respects, a year is a long time. So I have found it important to break down the goals I set for myself into bite-sized, ninety-day mini-goals. I also use this time to reflect on what I learned regarding what I did and did not achieve in the previous period. This knowledge becomes invaluable for the next ninety days and allows me to continually improve and make course corrections.

➲ Now, It's Your Turn

Complete this exercise in the chart below or in the workbook you downloaded from www.KeepAnyPromise.com/workbook.

1. In Column A, list the life categories you defined earlier.

2. In Column B, list the Annual Goals you defined in Chapter 15.

3. In Column C, identify what you would like to achieve in the next ninety days in order to help you meet your annual goals.

4. In Column D, define the key task or tasks that will help you reach each milestone.

	Column A	Column B	Column C	Column D
	Life category	Annual goal	In the next 90 days, what are the key milestones I want to achieve?	What key tasks do I need to set for myself to meet my goals?
1				
2				
3				
4				
5				
6				
7				
8				
9				
10				

This worksheet is contained within the free, downloadable workbook at www.KeepAnyPromise.com/workbook.

When you complete this exercise, share it with your close family and friends, and take the time to celebrate your many successes as they occur.

At the end of each ninety-day period, take stock of where you are and what you need to do for the upcoming period. This reflection will help you as you set the milestones and tasks for the upcoming period.

Complete the following chart in as much detail as possible. Use the free workbook you downloaded from www.KeepAnyPromise.com/workbook for your convenience.

	Column A	Column B	Column C	Column D	Column E
	Life categories	What did I achieve over the last three months?	What did I not achieve, and why?	In the next 90 days, what are the key milestones I want to achieve?	What key tasks do I need to set for myself to meet my goals?
1					
2					
3					
4					
5					
6					
7					
8					
9					
10					

Chapter 17:

What Will You Achieve in the Next Month?

A determined person will do more with a pen and paper than a lazy person will accomplish with a personal computer.

—*Catherine Pulsifer*

I have found it incredibly useful to think about each month individually because it helps give me an immediate road map for the short term. At the start of each month, take a few minutes to review your life categories and goals, and schedule chunks of time in your calendar for activities that will help you slowly but surely attain your goals. By doing so, you will find that you utilize your time optimally and minimize time-wasters.

I have found the format below to be particularly helpful. For each week, in each major area of your life or each major project that you may have underway, define the outcomes you would like to achieve. I have provided an example for one personal promise for one month that I hope will serve as a guide.

MONTH: Nov 1–Nov 30, 2007				
Health/ fitness	Week 1: Nov 1–Nov 8	Week 2: Nov 9–Nov 15	Week 3: Nov 16–Nov 22	Week 4: Nov 23–Nov 29
Get to dream weight: 158 lbs	· Get more vegetarian and fruit-focused in eating · Drink up to 2 liters of water per day · Walk 30km	· Get more vegetarian and fruit-focused in eating · Drink up to 2 liters of water per day · Walk 30km · Investigate Vitamix	· Get more vegetarian and fruit-focused in eating · Drink up to 2 liters of water per day · Walk 35km · Get iPod so that solitary walks are more pleasant	· Get more vegetarian and fruit-focused in eating · Drink up to 2 liters of water per day · Walk 40km · Set up iPod

➲ Now, It's Your Turn

Ideally, complete this exercise in the workbook that you downloaded from www.KeepAnyPromise.com/workbook.

In Column A, list your Life Categories. Refer to your goals and the key milestones and tasks that you identified in Chapter 16 for the next three months. Break these key tasks down into smaller outcomes you would like to see yourself achieve each week.

	Life category	Week 1: _____	Week 2: _____	Week 3: _____	Week 4: _____
MONTH/YEAR: _____					
1					
2					
3					
4					
5					
6					
7					
8					
9					
10					

Soon, just about everything you do will be focused on the goals you defined. The thousand and one distractions that lurk around every corner will be easy to avoid, guilt-free. Even things that you "have to do," if tied carefully to your purpose and goals, will suddenly have much more meaning.

At the end of each month, take a few minutes to answer the questions below. Your answers might just amaze you!

1. **What I have accomplished this month (my Wins!)**

    Celebrate/Compare against intended results.

    _____

    _____

    _____

    _____

    _____

    _____

2. **What I intended to do but didn't get done, and why**

    Acknowledge any lack of success.

    _____

    _____

    _____

    _____

    _____

    _____

    What is the gift or blessing in not having accomplished what I set out to do?

    _____

    _____

    _____

    _____

3. **What opportunities are available to me right now?**

There are always opportunities available in this abundant world. Sometimes, we just have to think hard.

_____

_____

_____

_____

_____

_____

4. **The breakthrough results I intend to achieve this month**

To get to your intended goal, it is essential that you make progress in small steps along the way. It is also important not to confuse activity with results. Yes, activity often precedes results, but keep your eye on the results you want to achieve, and try to make the results as big as possible. Think carefully about the words "breakthrough results I intend" above.

_____

_____

_____

_____

_____

_____

_____

5. What do I promise myself to *accomplish* next month?

List the activities, and ensure that you have included them with as much detail as possible below.

_____

_____

_____

_____

_____

_____

This worksheet is contained within the free, downloadable workbook at www.KeepAnyPromise.com/workbook.

Chapter 18:

What Would Make for a Fantastic Week?

The future cannot be predicted, but futures can be invented.
Only those who dare to fail greatly can ever achieve greatly.

—*Dennis Gabor*

A t the start of each week, review your monthly plan, and plan out your week so that you spend as much time as possible on those items that keep you on purpose. I have found that the color-coded weekly schedule I maintain in Microsoft Outlook gives me a great overall perspective on ensuring a balanced week. I have learned over time to work with my schedule in the following way.

1. Recurring items such as meditation, exercise, sleep, major celebratory events, vacations that can be planned ahead, and anything else really important is blocked off at the start of the year.

2. Each week, I can readily identify the time I have available, and I divide up my week with activities aimed at the outcomes I have outlined in the previous chapter, based on the monthly plan I developed.

3. I try and schedule one twenty-four-hour period when I am not working—no work calls, no e-mail, no meetings, and no cell phone pick-up unless it's personal/family. I find that this gives me the freedom to think creatively, something that is often difficult to achieve when

I am in the midst of carrying out activities. Need proof? Think of the last time you had a great idea at your desk versus while on vacation, on a walk, during a brainstorming session, etc.

4. A trick I have learned is to focus on the most difficult or unpleasant task or outcome first. Things rarely take as long as one thinks, or turn out as badly as one imagines. But the energy from accomplishing something difficult early in the day charges me up for the rest of the day.

5. Finally, I try and focus on achieving two or three key outcomes per day. This way, I can schedule these chunks of time into my calendar and focus on the really important things in my life.

Perhaps this way of organizing your week might sound radical. With your daily pressures, this approach may seem difficult at first. But if you persevere, you will eventually find that you lead a calm, on-purpose life; that you achieve much, much more; that you enjoy each week; and that your energy actually increases exponentially. One added benefit is that after almost forty years, I have given up making to-do lists, and surprisingly, I am much more productive and much calmer, even in the midst of very busy days.

Try it for just four weeks, and you will be amazed at how fantastic your weeks turn out.

Chapter 19:

Seven Magical Questions to Bring Fulfillment to Each Day

There are many fine things you mean to do some day, under what you think will be more favorable circumstances. But the only time that is yours is the present. Each day comes bearing gifts. Untie the knots.

—*Grenville Kleisher*

O ur lives are the sum of our days, just like a building is the sum of its bricks or stone. If each day is a wonderful, powerful, beautiful day, we will have created a wonderful life.

In the same way that the planning you are undertaking is essential to charting your life's journey, living each day to the fullest, living in the now, is vital to a great life.

Many people keep a daily journal to record their day. I found that when I began doing so in a purposeful manner, it completely changed my outlook on life. Now, at the **end** of each day, I ask myself the questions listed below, and I end the day by envisioning a fantastic tomorrow, which then manifests itself almost unfailingly. I have thought carefully about why this is so. I believe it derives from three factors.

First, when we sleep, our subconscious mind, which I feel is even more powerful than the conscious mind, kicks into gear. So each morning, solutions to challenges, big and small, usually present themselves, because the mind has been working on these when we sleep.

Second, in thinking ahead, we invariably do the preparation necessary to achieve a great outcome. After all, we know that, in most cases, going into a situation well prepared is likely to yield far better outcomes. If you think about the next day being terrific, your mind will automatically focus on those things that you can do to improve the outcome.

Third, in envisioning a fantastic tomorrow, we learn to stop worrying about things, because we know they will happen as intended. If they don't, then there is some learning to be gained, and likely an even bigger opportunity will come rolling along (it *always* does).

So I encourage you to follow the proposed system for three weeks. I *know* you will see great results as you answer these simple questions every day. To make it easier for you to do so, you can download the free workbook at www.KeepAnyPromise.com/workbook.

1. Today, what made me happy?

Think of all the things that made you happy, and list them. They could be the beautiful sunrise, a child's smile, a connection you make with someone, the difference you made in someone's life, etc. You might be surprised to find that rarely does happiness come from gaining more possessions, or winning more: rather, happiness comes from just *being*!

▸▸	
▸▸	
▸▸	

2.   Today, what am I grateful for?

Instead of complaining about things (and who doesn't from time to time?), try being grateful for everything you have. Remember that the majority of people in the world likely have far, far less to be grateful for than you do. Gratitude is also an acceptance of divine grace, and the more you are thankful for your divine grace, the more of it you will attract.

▸▸	
▸▸	
▸▸	

3.   Today, what were my most precious lessons?

Life is full of lessons, some small, some big. Every day, we learn something from the "good" things that happen to us to and the "bad" things that happen to us. Write down your lessons, for you and your spirit are your best teachers. Then review these lessons once a week. You will be amazed by how much you learned and how you can use these lessons to stay true to your life's purpose.

▸▸	
▸▸	
▸▸	

4.   Today, what were my good deeds?

This is usually the most difficult question for me to answer. Not that I don't live a life helping people, contributing to various causes, etc. But my definition of a good deed is something that I went out of my way to do for someone else, with no expectation of gain.

▶▶	
▶▶	
▶▶	

5.   Today, what was important to me?

My experience has been that reaching milestones, targets, acquiring new customers, etc., is important to me. Previously, I had viewed these areas as defining my happiness, and when I did not succeed at something, I was invariably miserable. Never mind that I could learn something from the exercise. Never mind that it was a near-impossible target for most people to achieve. Never mind that I could have been second or third, or achieved partial success. It was all or nothing for me, and this made me a very miserable person to be with whenever I suffered what I considered a "loss." So keep perspective on life, and pay careful attention to distinguish that which is merely important from that which is truly vital for your feelings of happiness: it is all too easy to confuse the two. Below, define what was important to you.

▶▶	
▶▶	
▶▶	

6. Today, what did I do to move me closer towards my goals?

As you reflect on each day, think about the goals that you have outlined for yourself, and ask yourself honestly how what you did today helped you stay on track with one or more goals. Your target is to eventually live a life of purpose, focused entirely on reaching, one step at a time, the awe-inspiring, long-term goals you have outlined for yourself.

▶▶	
▶▶	
▶▶	

7. Tomorrow, what will I achieve to make my life even more outstanding?

Every day, I visualize what my next day will be like and what outcomes I will achieve, and I simply prescribe an amazing day for my next day. A funny thing happens: that is exactly how the vast majority of days turn out.

As I mentioned previously, I have found it to be particularly helpful to focus my day on the two or three most important outcomes I wish to achieve. I then allocate as much time as possible to these two or three outcomes in my calendar.

When things go differently, I now have the wisdom to not rail against the world, but to accept that grace and know that there is always a reason why things are the way they are. I know that there is likely a lesson from which I can learn (and which often teaches me to take increasing responsibility for my outcomes in life).

So go ahead and prescribe a fantastic day, every day, and watch it unfold, day by day.

▶▶	
▶▶	
▶▶	

Chapter 20:

How Can I Maximize My Energy?

Energy is the essence of life. Every day you decide how you're going to use it by knowing what you want and what it takes to reach that goal, and by maintaining focus.

—*Oprah Winfrey*

In order to have the best shot at reaching my huge goals, I realized that I needed to maximize my energy levels. So I did what all smart people do: I studied experts in the subject area, i.e., people who had tons of energy every day.

The most influential example has been my friend and one-time colleague Keith Rieger. He follows a system based on the *Fit for Life* program by Harvey and Marilyn Diamond. Keith is a long-distance runner, and no ordinary one at that: he just ran the Western States 100 Mile Running Race, one of the world's toughest races (see Chapter 8). A strict adherent of this program is Tony Robbins, and if you ever had the pleasure of seeing him give a high-energy seminar with unflagging energy for hours, you would be convinced. I also talked to many others, and then tried a number of different things to arrive at the system below.

You might be thinking: I have tried many other systems; none of them worked, so why will this one? All I can offer you is my example: I lost forty pounds in four months and have kept the majority off for four years so far.

But most importantly, I am full of energy every day. I sleep five hours a night and awake refreshed.

The system is simple. Try it for three weeks—you'll be surprised at the results. But if this does not work for you, then come up with any other system that does, based on the following principles:

1. Sit in quiet contemplation every day and let stillness invade your life; just be, for even a few minutes a day

2. Exercise regularly: walking is safest

3. Drink lots of water

4. Eat well, but, in order to aid digestion, avoid mixing protein and carbohydrates

5. Sleep deep (can be hard to do, but aim to be child-like in your sleep)

6. Avoid "energy sappers"—people or situations

Below is *my* plan. Adapt it as you see fit, keeping in mind the above principles.

1. Meditation/prayer

I start my day with meditation and prayer, which gives me perspective on what is truly important in the short time we are on this journey on Earth. It also starts off my day helping me feel connected to my Creator. There are many forms of meditation. All of them generally aim to still the mind from the daily chatter our mind encounters in some way, shape, or form. So do whatever works for you.

2. Exercise

Having exercised the mind (for meditation is hard work), I normally walk briskly in the morning, and I try and complete thirty to fifty kilometers a week. I hit this target often through longer walks on weekends. While I would love to play squash or badminton again, these games are severely contra-indicated for my back. I stretch carefully, and I am ready to tackle the day's many challenges.

3. Water

I drink two to three liters of water a day. I drink some of the water with lime or lemon to alkalize the body better. Cucumber slices are also a good way to alkalize your body, helping reduce the impact of the many acids we consume through breads, meats, etc.

4. Balanced eating

I eat according to the circadian rhythm of the body, using principles articulated in *Fit for Life*. This ensures that I am eating to gain energy and to nourish the body.

Morning	Fruit only—easy to digest, gives me maximum energy
Snacks	More fruit plus dried fruit; e.g., raisins, apricots
Lunchtime	Vegetables; e.g., soup/salad—nourishing and gives me energy
Snacks	Carrots/celery
Around 4-ish	A carbohydrate; e.g., a bagel (not with cheese)
Dinner	I try and eat early, before 7 p.m. on most days. I do not mix carbohydrates and protein wherever possible: both foods are hardest to digest, so it drains my body of energy, and I feel sluggish after eating such a meal. So I pair a carbohydrate with vegetables, and pair proteins (fish or other seafood, lentils, etc.) with vegetables too
3 hours after dinner	Fruit for dessert
Before going to bed	Hot water, with the juice of ½ to 1 lemon—allows me to sleep well and is great for detoxifying the body

So what have I eliminated? Tea/coffee, dairy products for the most part, fried food, rich desserts, and fruit juice concentrates for the most part.

Do I "cheat"? Yes. I see them as treats. When I was trying to lose weight, I allowed myself one treat per week in the first month, two in the second month, three in the third month, and four from the fourth month onwards. For me, a treat usually consists of a bit of chocolate after a meal—I have a small piece (or two) of 70 percent cocoa dark chocolate.

The net effect: I am rarely hungry, and the food I eat leaves me nourished, highly energized, and feeling lean.

5.   Sleep

Because I go to sleep after completing my daily journal and ideally after reading something inspiring, I find I sleep very deeply and can awake refreshed in five hours. I found it vital to cut out watching TV, especially the news later in the evening, so consequently, the TV is rarely on in our household. Truth be told, I would rather not sleep at all, as there is so much I would like to do in my lifetime. But I know that sleep helps repair my body, so I try and follow a consistent sleep routine.

6.   Energy sappers

Often, one encounters people or situations that are energy sappers. It could be someone who is excessively negative about the world, or about what you are doing. Avoid such people, or reduce your time with them if you can't avoid them.

Work situations can be energy sappers. Watch out for such situations actively, and do your best to put an end to energy-sapping activities. (Hint: if you stay true to your life's purpose, you will almost always be able to deal with such situations.)

To maximize waiting periods—doctor's office, delayed flights, etc.—always keep reading material or a small diary/journal with you, and make the best use of such downtime. Start seeing downtime as a blessing.

7. **Goal and purpose review**

To stay on purpose amidst the hundreds of distractions every day and week, it is vital that you focus on your purpose and goals. So take a few minutes each week, each month, each quarter, and again annually to plan out your life. Isn't your life worth it?

Evaluate your current lifestyle and energy level, and then pick as many items from the above list as you wish to start with. If you wish to have more energy, make some lifestyle changes.

PART 3:

The Big Life Questions

Many of us spend half our time wishing for things we could have if we didn't spend half our time wishing.

—*Alexander Woollcott*

You have been on an exciting journey so far, one of achievement and self-discovery. Congratulations! With these achievements behind you, you are ready to tackle some deeper issues that will help provide a wonderful framework for your life.

Get ready, for you will be asking yourself some tough questions, but keep in mind that the answers to these questions lie deep within you. Just think long and hard, and as you do so, often the answers will appear from least expected sources.

Chapter 21:

Are You Ready for a Simple but Tough Quiz?

The ultimate measure of a man is not where he stands in moments of comfort and convenience, but where he stands at times of challenge and controversy.

—*Martin Luther King*

I am hopeful that you will find the results of this simple quiz enlightening. Read each question carefully, close your eyes for fifteen seconds to think about your answer, and then place a tick in *one* of the three columns for each question. Add your scores based on the number of checks in each column. You can also complete this exercise online at www. KeepAnyPromise.com/lifequiz. Ideally, do both.

		Column 1	Column 2	Column 3
		Yes	No	Maybe
1	Have you clearly defined your purpose in life?			
2	Do you feel you are making a substantial difference in the world?			
2	Have you set huge goals with a long-term (20-year) time horizon?			
4	Are you making measurable progress towards your goals?			
5	Do you spend most of your time doing the things you absolutely love doing?			
6	Do you plan your days and your life to achieve what is most important to you?			
7	Are you continually grateful for what you have/are?			
8	Are you motivated each day to be the best person you can be?			
9	Do you pay regular, consistent attention to the people who matter most to you?			
10	Are you happy every day of your life?			
	Your score			

You can take this exercise and receive very valuable feedback online at www.KeepAnyPromise.com/lifequiz.

How to Interpret Your Score:

Seven or more ticks in Column 1: Many aspects of your life are in great shape; by focusing on the other areas a bit more, you will enjoy an incredible life.

Between four and seven ticks in Column 1: Many aspects of your life are in good shape, but you should consider paying much more attention to the items where you checked No or Maybe.

Zero to four ticks in Column 1: You have some heavy lifting to do before you feel satisfied with your life. This book and the simple exercises here, if followed regularly, will help you significantly increase satisfaction and happiness with your life.

Whatever your score, retake this quiz every few months, and you will be amazed at how rapidly your scores change from No or Maybe to Yes, once you complete the exercises in this book and begin to implement them consistently.

Now that it's clear what you need to do, it's time to get started on an exciting journey ... defining what makes you tick.

Chapter 22:

Your Values, or Who Are You at Your Core?

Trust in yourself. Your perceptions are far more accurate than you are willing to believe.

—*Claudia Black*

Before you proceed, it is important that you define your core values. This will help you better understand who you are and what *really* drives you. The work you do here is critical, so if you do only one exercise in this book, this should be it.

What is a value? In simple terms, values are those non-negotiable attributes that define who you are. Not who you think you should be or would like to be. But who you are, right now.

Let's look at the values of four famous figures: Mahatma Gandhi, Martin Luther King Jr., Mother Teresa, and Nelson Mandela.

Mahatma Gandhi was the pioneer of total non-violent resistance based on mass civil disobedience. He said:

"You might of course say that there can be no non-violent rebellion and there has been none known to history. Well, it is my ambition to provide an instance, and it is my dream that my country may win its freedom through non-violence. And, I would like to repeat to the world times without number, that I will not purchase my country's freedom at the cost of non-violence. My marriage to non-violence is such an absolute thing that I would rather commit suicide than be deflected from my position. I have not mentioned truth in this connection, simply because truth cannot be expressed excepting by non-violence."

His values came to be one of the strongest driving philosophies of the Indian independence movement and have inspired movements for civil rights and freedom across the world.

Martin Luther King Jr., the youngest recipient of the Nobel Peace Prize, said in his famous *I Have a Dream!* speech:

"I have a dream that one day this nation will rise up and live out the true meaning of its creed: 'We hold these truths to be self-evident, that all men are created equal.'

"I have a dream that one day on the red hills of Georgia, the sons of former slaves and the sons of former slave owners will be able to sit down together at the table of brotherhood.

"I have a dream that one day even the state of Mississippi, a state sweltering with the heat of injustice, sweltering with the heat of oppression, will be transformed into an oasis of freedom and justice.

"I have a dream that my four little children will one day live in a nation where they will not be judged by the color of their skin but by the content of their character.

"I have a dream today!"

Mother Teresa was defined by her desire to care for (in her own words) "… the hungry, the naked, the homeless, the crippled, the blind, the lepers, all those people who feel unwanted, unloved, uncared for throughout society, people that have become a burden to the society and are shunned by everyone."

Nelson Mandela said: "During my lifetime I have dedicated myself to this struggle of the African people. I have fought against white domination, and I have fought against black domination. I have cherished the ideal of a democratic and free society in which all persons live together in harmony and with equal opportunities. It is an ideal which I hope to live for and to achieve. But if it needs be, it is an ideal for which I am prepared to die."

Their values defined them and provided them a moral compass in turbulent times, sometimes over long periods, as in the case of Nelson Mandela's imprisonment.

➲ Now, It's Your Turn

You might want to do the following exercise with a friend or loved one. You don't have to share the results of the exercise if you don't want to, but you will undoubtedly find it even more valuable if you do, since sharing the results will help you define your values even better. To gain maximum value, proceed step by step.

Step 1

1. Sit in a quiet room, close your eyes, and slow down your breathing.
2. Think about the *highest* point in your life. Think about what it felt like. What emotions did you go through? How did it truly feel? Think hard about every aspect of this high point in your life. What else did you experience? Take your time, do not rush. Open your eyes.
3. List the highest point in the chart below, or in the workbook that you downloaded from www.KeepAnyPromise.com/workbook.
4. In Column A, list everything that went through your mind. Is there anything else that you can recall? Anything you want to add?
5. In Column B, reduce everything to one descriptive word per line.

Below is my list of emotions and thoughts when I was at the highest point in my life. I share them so that you have an example to help you.

	The highest point in my life was in January 2005, when I was at the top of Mt. Kilimanjaro	
	Column A	**Column B**
	My thoughts and feelings at the highest point in my life	**Summarized in one word**
1	Overcoming what I never thought I could	Triumph
2	Very connected with nature	Awestruck
3	Vindication of health progress	Healthy
4	Incredible sense of accomplishment	Exhilaration
5	Purpose unfolding	Purposeful
6	Spiritually connected	Connected
7	Gratitude for the help I had received	Grateful
8	Not a quitter	Able
9	Dogged determination	Perseverance
10	Had the discipline to stick with the climb	Disciplined

➲ Now, It's Your Turn

One of the highest points in my life was _____

	Column A	Column B
	My thoughts and feelings at the highest point in my life	Summarized in one word
1		
2		
3		
4		
5		
6		
7		
8		
9		
10		
11		
12		
13		
14		
15		
16		
17		
18		
19		
20		

This worksheet is contained within the free, downloadable workbook at www.KeepAnyPromise.com/workbook.

Step 2

1. Sit in a quiet room, close your eyes, and slow down your breathing.

2. Think about the *lowest* point in your life. Think about what it felt like. What emotions did you go through? How did it truly feel? Think hard about every aspect of this low point in your life. What else did you experience? Take your time, do not rush. Open your eyes.

3. List the lowest point in the chart on the next page, or in the workbook that you downloaded from www.KeepAnyPromise.com/workbook.

4. In Column A, list everything that went through your mind. Is there anything else that you can recall? Anything you want to add?

5. In Column B, reduce everything to one descriptive word per line.

6. In Column C, think of the opposite to that word. For example, if you experienced Sadness, the opposite would be Joy. Write it down.

Below is **my** list of emotions and thoughts when I was at the lowest point in my life. I share them so that you have an example to help you.

	The lowest point in my life was in early 2002, when I had no desire to live and wanted the deep physical and emotional pain in my life to permanently stop		
	Column A	Column B	Column C
	My thoughts and feelings at the lowest point in my life	Summarized in one word	The opposite of this word
1	Spiritually disconnected	Disconnected	Connected
2	Alone and lonely	Alone	Embraced
3	No world contribution	Taker	Giver
4	Complete helplessness	Helplessness	Self-sufficient
5	Not understood	Misunderstood	Understood
6	No clear way out	Dead-end	Clarity
7	Deep physical pain	Painful	Pain-free
8	Highly stressed	Stressed	Calm
9	Anger with the world	Angry	Forgiving
10	Emotional pain	Hurt	Joy
11	Frequent sleeplessness	Sleeplessness	Restful
12	Altered state, by medication	Numb	Vibrant
13	Weak and debilitated	Weak	Strong

➲ Now, It's Your Turn

	One of the lowest points in my life was _____ _____		
	Column A	Column B	Column C
	My thoughts and feelings at the lowest point in my life	Summarized in one word	The opposite of this word
1			
2			
3			
4			
5			
6			
7			
8			
9			
10			
11			
12			
13			
14			
15			
16			
17			
18			
19			
20			

This worksheet is contained within the free, downloadable workbook at www.KeepAnyPromise.com/workbook.

Congratulations for being so honest with yourself.

From the list of values in Column B from the highest point in your life (see page 130) and Column C of this just-completed exercise, the lowest point of your life, select a *combined total* of ten items that are most important to you, as guides for how to behave or as components of a valued way of life. Put these in order of importance below.

The ten most important values that define me are:

1.	
2.	
3.	
4.	
5.	
6.	
7.	
8.	
9.	
10.	

Is this an inspiring set of values? Do these values exemplify who you are at your best? Keep these wonderful values in front of you as you work on the next chapter.

Chapter 23:

The Big Question:
What Is the Purpose of Your Life?

> *To be what we are and to become what we are capable of becoming, is the only end of life.*
>
> —*Robert Louis Stevenson*

I f you are in the 2 percent of people who can clearly describe your life's purpose, bravo! Many people struggle with achieving a clear life purpose, sometimes all their lives. But don't panic: complete the simple exercise in this and the chapters to follow, and your life's true purpose will emerge.

Why is it important to have a clear life purpose? Simply, it provides an essential framework for your life. As Marianne Williamson states so eloquently, "The purpose of our lives is to give birth to the best that is within us."

Os Guinness in *The Call: Finding and Fulfilling the Central Purpose of Your Life* said, "The search for the purpose of life is one of the deepest of our experiences as human beings. Deep in our hearts, we all want to find and fulfill a purpose bigger than ourselves." Guinness adds, "For each of us the real purpose is personal and passionate: to know what we are to do and why."

Your life purpose should therefore be broad, inspiring, and, hopefully, articulate the huge impact you would like to make during your lifetime. Why? Because each one of us can do so, as you learned from the twelve diverse role models in Part 1 of this book. In essence, defining your life purpose will help you unleash your true potential.

To start, think about three of your heroes and summarize their life purpose below.

	Hero	Life purpose
1		
2		
3		

Next, write out the exact obituary *you* would like to represent your accomplishments at the end of your life. Be as specific as possible. (Review any good newspaper to see examples of well-written, inspiring obituaries.) What exactly would you want written about you to summarize your life? What would move, touch, and inspire the many friends, family, and strangers who will one day be reading your obituary? Keep in mind the ten most important values you defined in the previous chapter.

Obituary for (your name) _____ at the end of your life at age

_____

_____

_____

_____

_____

_____

_____

_____

_____

_____

_____

_____

_____

_____

_____

_____

_____

_____

_____

_____

_____

Reduce this obituary to ten, twenty, thirty, or forty words that you can memorize and repeat at the drop of a hat. That is your life purpose. To help you, here is my own life purpose, arrived at through the same process:

My purpose in life is to get ever closer to my Creator through sharing my wonderful blessings to make an extraordinary difference in the world.

If you would like to do further work in this area, please see the e-book by Stacey Mayo listed at www.KeepAnyPromise.com/resources. It contains

very practical exercises that will help you define or refine your life purpose.

➲ Now, It's Your Turn

Complete the section below and then revisit it every six months for the
next two years to refine it:

I am (your name) _____ and my life's purpose is:

_____

_____

_____

_____

While this is a great start, defining your purpose is not a simple matter,
because you evolve and the world evolves—change is the only constant in
our lives.

In the next chapter, you will define the first of your large, twenty-year
goals and start tracking progress on one key goal. Through an iterative process, you will gain more and more clarity about your life's purpose and over
time will likely come back and refine the life purpose you defined. That's
normal. Just *trust* your all-knowing instinct as you embark on this exhilarat-
ing journey toward taking charge of your future. At this point, you may be
thinking: how or why should I just trust? The answer is simple. I believe we
are all born in perfection. Over time, we succumb to the influences of the
world. Along the way, we learn to start doubting, and we stop trusting the
perfect instincts with which we were born.

Our inner voices ask: "Am I good enough? Will I be able to do this?
What if I fail? What will people think?" Yet if we examine our core, we all
have a spark of divinity that is our essence, and as we come to recognize

this inner spirit and learn to trust it, we are able to still those doubting inner voices.

In the next chapter, you will complete an exercise that very few people ever undertake: setting twenty-year goals. I hope you will find this exercise as mind-opening as I did and that it will help you to think *big*.

Chapter 24:

Setting Twenty-year Goals:
The Value in Thinking *Big*!

> *Twenty years from now, you will be more disappointed by the things you didn't do than by the ones you did. So throw off the bowlines. Sail away from the safe harbor. Catch the trade winds in your sails. Explore. Dream. Discover.*
>
> —*Mark Twain*

Now that you have defined a clear purpose for your life, perhaps for the first time, it is important to make the attainment of your vision possible.

The best way I have found is to define three or four big twenty-year goals, so that you have a long-term framework to guide you. I highly recommend twenty-year goals because the long timeframe provides the freedom to think *big*. These goals can be whatever you wish, but they should be clear, measurable, and *huge*. After all, you have two decades to achieve these goals, so time is on your side!

We know that our minds have infinite capacity, and they like to be challenged. So if you set small goals, your mind takes a big yawn and is not motivated to undertake much change. Instead, set *huge* goals, ones that on the surface make you want to shake your head in disbelief. Then watch your mind stretch, because it is now motivated to do what it does best—*think hard.* It's actually quite easy.

Remember Marianne Williamson's words at the start of this book. As you define your life purpose and your twenty-year goals, let *your* light shine.

My twenty-year goals are listed below to help you:

1. Provide the opportunity for five million (yes, *five* million) individuals to transform their lives in the way mine has been transformed.

2. Consult to twenty non-profits in order to help them make huge leaps in their goals and fulfill their missions more smoothly.

3. Make annual charitable contributions of at least 25 percent of profits.

4. Continue my personal transformation (in health and fitness, spirituality, emotions, mental outlook, personal attributes, generosity, volunteerism, and relationships).

➲ Now, It's Your Turn

Complete the exercise below, or use the workbook that you downloaded from www.KeepAnyPromise.com/workbook.

My outrageous, top three or four twenty-year goals are … (*Remember:* make your goals as specific and measurable and huge as possible, so you are left gasping when you share these goals with your family and friends)

1) _____

_____

_____

_____

2) _____

_____

_____

_____

3) _____

_____

_____

_____

4) _____

_____

_____

_____

This worksheet is contained within the free, downloadable workbook at www.KeepAnyPromise.com/workbook.

So … do these huge goals scare you? Do you think they will inspire you and others? And are you unsure how you will achieve them, even though you know you have two decades in which to do so? Don't worry; the next few chapters are designed to inspire you as you set out on your journey to achieving these goals.

It's time now to take the ten values you defined, your life purpose, and your top four goals and put them all together in a comprehensive manner, using the chart on the next page or in the workbook you downloaded. You will find that as you do so, you might need to make adjustments to either your ten values, your life purpose, or your top four goals so that they tie in to each other in a well-integrated manner. Feel free to do so.

Summary

Insert life purpose here from Chapter 23									
Insert 1st 20-year goal here			Insert 2nd 20-year goal here		Insert 3rd 20-year goal here			Insert 4th 20-year goal here	
1	2	3	4	5	6	7	8	9	10

Insert top 10 values from Chapter 22 in the cells above

This worksheet is contained within the free, downloadable workbook at www.KeepAnyPromise.com/workbook.

Chapter 25:

If You Had Fifty Wishes for Your Lifetime, What Would They Be?

Do not go where the path may lead, go instead where there is no path and leave a trail.

—*Ralph Waldo Emerson*

L et's now try an exercise that I am sure will be lots of fun for you, as it has been for me and others. Let's define fifty wishes for your life. I promise you that the exercise below will make you think outside the box. Here are some questions for you to consider.

1. Who would you love to meet?

2. Where would you like to travel?

3. What would you like to stop doing?

4. What fun or crazy things would you like to do?

5. What changes in the world would you like to be a part of?

6. How would you like to relate to your friends and family?

Use the chart on page 146 or the one you downloaded from www.KeepAnyPromise.com/workbook.

1. In Column A, list everything that you would love to do in your lifetime if you could. Don't worry about limiting factors such as time, money, and so on—just dream. And don't worry about order, timing, or priorities. Just let the ideas flow.

2. In Column B, list the year in which you would like to accomplish these wishes.

3. In Column C and for the next three years, list the month for each item.

4. In Column D, list the current status of each item. Review this every ninety days. This will help you track your successes.

You will be surprised at what you come up with. One item on my wish list was to write a bestseller. I was thinking of fiction, something along the lines of John Grisham's novels. This triggered a thought: why not share my goal-setting and life experiences to create another, much more meaningful type of bestseller? And so was born the inspirational guide that you are reading.

Finally, don't worry if you can't think of fifty items that have meaning to you. This is a work in progress that you can update over time. Have fun listing these wishes and then actually seeing them come true in your life.

I have listed some personal examples below to spur your thinking.

#	Column A	Column B	Column C	Column D
	50 things I would like to do in my life	Year	Month	Status
1	Take a BMW driving course	2008	November	
2	Hike to Base Camp Everest	2009	October	Trip being planned
3	Complete Grouse Grind in Vancouver in two hours	2008	Fall	
4	Cut a CD of recitations	2008	February	In progress
5	Visit my birthplace: Pemba, near Zanzibar, Tanzania	2006	March	Completed
6	Ride in a helicopter	2006	October	Completed
7	Sit perfectly still for half an hour in meditation	2006	December	Completed
8	See Aliya graduate from Wellesley	2006	May	Completed
9	See Amaan graduate from Georgetown	2008	May	Completed
10	Be a grandparent			
11	Own a dog			
12	Learn to salsa dance			
13	Fund 1,000 bedkits per year in 5 years (from 130 in 2006)	2011	June	In progress
14	Learn to swim properly			
15	See the Dalai Lama in person	2007	October	Completed
16	Learn Spanish at a conversational level			
17	Hike the Andes and see the Lost City of the Incas, Machu Picchu in Peru	2007	August	Completed

This is a sample of the many wonderful items on my list. A funny thing happened as I wrote this list: opportunities started popping up for me to undertake the items on the list, even ones I had not thought possible. Wayne Dyer's *Power of Intention* was at work (see Resources).

➲ Now, It's Your Turn

#	Column A 50 things I would like to do in my life	Column B Year	Column C Month	Column D Status
1				
2				
3				
4				
5				
6				
7				
8				
9				
10				
11				
12				
13				
14				
15				
16				
17				
18				
19				
20				
21				
22				

#	Column A	Column B	Column C	Column D
	50 things I would like to do in my life	Year	Month	Status
23				
24				
25				
26				
27				
28				
29				
30				
31				
32				
33				
34				
35				
36				
37				
38				
39				
40				
41				
42				
43				
44				

#	Column A 50 things I would like to do in my life	Column B Year	Column C Month	Column D Status
45				
46				
47				
48				
49				
50				

This worksheet is contained within the free, downloadable workbook at www.KeepAnyPromise.com/workbook.

If you started or completed this list, well done! How did it feel listing these wishes?

If you are feeling adventurous, you might wish to put together a fifty-slide PowerPoint presentation: one slide with relevant pictures and/or text for each wish. See if you can make these fifty images into a screen saver for your desktop or laptop, so you constantly see these wishes. Visualization is really powerful in helping you achieve your goals. As these wishes come true, you can replace the image that you use to visualize with one that depicts your actual accomplishment!

Having had what I hope is a lot of fun (with lots of crazy ideas that you might never have imagined until now), in the next chapter let's look at how you can go about attracting what you want.

Chapter 26:

How Can I Attract What I Want?

> *The true nature of our ground state and that of the universe is that it is a field of all possibilities. ... From this level it is possible to create anything. This field is our own essential nature. ... It is our inner self. It is also called the absolute, and it is the ultimate authority.*

> —*Deepak Chopra*

The first step is to achieve clarity about what you are seeking. After all, if you present a fuzzy picture of what you want, or no picture at all, how can you expect the universe to respond appropriately? I found that when I have clarity about what I want, the universe has a very logical way of manifesting my thoughts. So the more vividly we can picture our goals, the greater the chances we will achieve what we desire.

While the process of goal-setting outlined in this inspirational guide is in many ways a linear one, many of us are right-brained, emotional thinkers. So enjoy the exercise below. You will create an Attraction Board that allows you to put in pictures that which you have expressed so far in words.

1. Have your **three-year goals** and **Fifty Wishes** lists in front of you.

2. Gather a large pile of glossy magazines that you enjoy.

3. Go through these and snip images or headline text that relate in some way to your goals. (For example, if your goal is to be retired as a couple at fifty and lead an active physical life, then you might wish to find a picture of a healthy, vibrant couple walking on the beach, hiking, etc. If your goal is to spend a month exploring one of twenty different countries in each of the next twenty years, then you might wish to collect images from each of these countries.)

4. Take a large poster board or large sheet of paper and start pasting the images and text in a manner that distinguishes one goal from another.

5. Fill up the entire large page, and then hang this up somewhere prominent where you and others will see it.

6. Sit down with your Attraction Board annually, as you examine your three-year goals.

7. Every three years, repeat this exercise—you will be amazed at how much you achieve.

8. To maximize your fun, do this with a group (family, friends, or co-workers); each person completes his or her own Attraction Board.

If you can dream it, if you can visualize it, you *can* achieve it. In the next chapter, you will learn about a very important concept that will help you remove roadblocks standing between you and your goals.

Chapter 27:

Can You Truly Forgive?

To forgive is the highest, most beautiful form of love. In return, you will receive untold peace and happiness.

—*Robert Muller*

One of the key things that holds many people back is their inability to forgive: to forgive themselves, parents, children, other family members, former employers, etc. Often, people hold onto long-term, festering, and sometimes overblown ills, errors, and "sins." This is analogous to trying to climb a hill, possibly very steep, and being weighed down with *tons* of baggage. Who in their right mind would not seek an alternative to this situation?

Where does forgiveness start? I have learned that it must start with oneself. So think hard about your life so far, and systematically examine the ups and downs, including your relationships with each and every person of significance in your life. Go back as far as you can remember. Write down all the contacts and encounters and situations along your life journey. Then think carefully about whether you are carrying any baggage from each situation for which you blame yourself. Whatever you uncover, resolve to forgive yourself. Whatever happened and whatever role you played, keep in mind that it was:

a)   In the past

b)   Likely overblown in your mind

c)   A learning and growing opportunity

Unless you can learn to forgive yourself, you will be blocked in the progress you can make in your own life.

I learned that I needed to forgive myself for not being as good a spouse as I aspired to be; for not being a better parent and more available when our children were younger; for being too strict with the children when they were younger; for not achieving the financial targets I had set for myself within the timeframes I had set; for not spending as much time as I would have liked with my parents; for not being as good a brother as possible to my sister (with whom I have had a tumultuous relationship, but whom I love deeply). I resolved to put all this behind me. How, you ask?

Well, in each case, I talked things over with the other person, shared what I needed to forgive myself for, and asked for their forgiveness. The sense of love and closure that I was quickly able to apply to all these situations removed the baggage I was carrying.

Was it tough? You bet. Was it worth it? You bet, for I ended up with much stronger relationships.

Forgiveness is an essential part of living life to the fullest; in so doing, we actually help ourselves as much as those we are forgiving.

But what if the person is no longer accessible to you, or if the person has passed away in the meantime? Then have an imaginary conversation with them; know that most people are very forgiving, and visualize them forgiving you. But put closure to such situations, or they will weigh you down.

One of the most powerful examples of forgiveness comes from the Dalai Lama, in an interview with Victor Chan in the *Wisdom of Forgiveness*. "So being able to forgive your enemies can make a difference to one's spiritual progress?" Victor Chan asked the Dalai Lama. "Yes, yes, there is no doubt," he replied. "It's crucial. It's one of the most important things. It can change one's life. To reduce hatred and other destructive emotions, you must develop their opposites—compassion and kindness. If you have strong compassion, strong respect for others, then forgiveness is much easier. Mainly for this reason: I do not want to harm another. Forgiveness allows you to be in touch with these positive emotions. This will help with spiritual development. ... I pay special attention to the Chinese—especially those doing terrible things to the Tibetans. ... As I meditate, I breathe in all their poisons—hatred, fear, cruelty. Then I breathe out. And I let all the good things come out, like compassion, forgiveness. I take inside my body all these bad things. Then I replace poisons with fresh air. Giving and taking. I take care not to blame—I don't blame the Chinese and I don't blame myself. The meditation is very effective, useful to reduce hatred, useful to cultivate forgiveness."

So think again about whom you need to forgive in order to move on with your life, and then just go ahead and do so consciously, in whatever way makes the most sense to you.

The next chapter is extremely important in helping you remove the most important barrier to most people's success: fear. Let it control you and you are guaranteed to live a life well below your potential. Overcome it, and you will soar.

Chapter 28:

Fear, the Biggest Impediment to Growth

"The longer you fail to believe in the power deep within you, the longer and stronger fear's hold on you will be."

—Author unknown

I n the last few chapters, you've come a long way and learned a lot about yourself. After completing the preceding exercises, you are well-equipped to achieve your goals and to keep *all* your promises. There is one more vital step I urge you to take: to help *sustain* positive outcomes in your life, read through this chapter very carefully, heed the lessons, and complete the exercises fully.

When we are born, we have no fear. Observe young children. They will want to climb over any obstacle in their path, touch everything, and, in short, do anything, because they have no fear. However our parents, in trying to protect us, gradually instill fear in us. From an early age, we are told "don't touch the fire," "don't go right to the edge," "be careful," etc. As a parent, I understand why we act the way we do: we are simply trying to protect our children from the many dangers we see in the world. But children and young adults who are exclusively taught not to take risks, even calculated ones, grow up to be risk-averse adults susceptible to fear-related internal messages that resonate loudly within as they face life's challenges.

155

Through our school and college and university years and beyond, we face many fears: of not being liked, not making friends, failing exams, choosing the "wrong" college, career, job, spouse, etc. Such fears can often become front and center in people's minds. And the media engenders even more fear: of war, of natural disasters, for personal safety, etc. It's no wonder then that many of us are paralyzed by fear, as I learned I was, because we have more than two decades of fear-related thinking drummed into us by the time we are in our twenties!

What happens in our late twenties, thirties, and forties? We realize we have to take risks to make progress in life, so we try and make them "calculated risks," i.e., taken after careful thought. Sometimes we succeed and sometimes we fail in our endeavors. But every time we fail, we become more risk averse, and we slow down our growth, at just the age when we have begun to gain the wisdom to more fully realize our potential.

Simultaneously, many people have not only a fear of failure, but often a fear of success. This causes us to "play small," in the words of Marianne Williamson. You may be wondering why anyone would be afraid of success. Think of the inner voices that whisper: "What will 'they' say (to our success)?"; "Be modest and don't show off"; "I don't deserve this success because I am not worth it"; "I am an imposter and someone will find out that I am really not that clever/smart/skillful, etc."; "Will my friends continue to be my friends if I am much more successful than they are?"; "Will I want them as my friends?"; "Will this mean that I am better than my parents, who may not have enjoyed such success?"

Some people also back off from success because they feel that once they succeed, there is nowhere to go but downhill from there, or because they feel they will need to continue to expend huge efforts to maintain their success. Such self-limiting thoughts are common, and they compound the fears described earlier.

And what about when we are in our fifties, sixties, and seventies? Other fears click in: of getting old, disease, being a burden on our families, having insufficient funds to enjoy retirement, and death, to name a few fears.

Sound like anyone you know? I had multiple fears, especially the fear of future success, in my forties, until I learned that unless I looked at fear differently, it would literally kill me.

So how can you go about dealing with *your* fears? It's actually quite easy if you follow the step-by-step process outlined here. Do your best to complete every exercise, no matter how challenging it may seem at first.

Step 1: Define your fears

What are your top fears? What keeps you awake at night? What fears are often at the back of your mind, eating away at you? These fears can range from tiny to enormous, but be assured that they are stopping you from growing, and they are having a major impact on your life. So think very hard and define your top ten fears below. And if you have a fear of commitment, just take a deep breath and start the list anyway. You can change the list later as you better understand your truest, deepest fears.

Here are some common fears. Do any of them fit in your top ten list?

- Change
- Commitment
- Confrontation
- Darkness
- Death
- Dependence
- Enclosed Spaces
- Failure
- Heights
- Ill-health
- Loneliness
- Losing control
- Losing independence
- Losing love
- Natural disasters
- Not measuring up
- Old age
- Other people's opinions
- Poverty
- Rejection
- Responsibility
- Success
- War

If you have any difficulty in coming up with a full list of your fears, think for a moment about whether any aspects of your daily behavior may be clues to your beliefs and, hence, your fears. Often, people indulge in self-sabotaging behavior, caused by something within them that is stronger than their desire to achieve their goal. This prevents them from doing the things they want to do or having the things they want to have. Here are some typical behaviors that pertain to many of the items above. Do any of these behaviors seem familiar?

1. Procrastinating often

2. Leaving projects half-finished

3. Worrying needlessly about things over which one has little control

4. Being constantly busy, but having little to show for results

5. Wanting to do everything yourself, because you feel only you can do it really well

If any of these behaviors sound like you, then you may be indulging in self-sabotaging behavior that is driven by your beliefs, in turn fuelled by your fears.

Please list your top ten fears in Column A below. In Column B, note how these manifest themselves in your life, which you may correlate with either the beliefs or behaviors that you observe.

	Column A	Column B
	My predominant fears are:	These fears appear in the following ways in my life (list beliefs you hold or behaviors you observe)
1		
2		
3		
4		
5		
6		
7		
8		
9		
10		

This worksheet is contained within the free, downloadable workbook at www.KeepAnyPromise.com/workbook.

By completing this exercise, you have taken a very important first step in dealing with fear: defining what you fear and beginning to understand how that fear might be showing up in your life.

Step 2: Embrace your fear

The Bible says, "The truth shall set you free." This first step you have taken along the fear-busting journey is the foundation for embracing your fear.

But how, exactly, do you go about embracing your fears? I discovered that there were at least three ways to embrace my fears, and that when I did so, I experienced incredible freedom.

Choose to face your fears. Instead of letting fear control me, I made up my mind that I would start controlling it. This meant that I was finally in charge of the solution and that I had taken complete responsibility for the situation in which I found myself. For example, when our business started suffering losses, at first I was petrified because this was occurring at the same time that our two children would be entering university, with its attendant costs. However, my business partner and I believed firmly that we had skills and value to offer to the right clients. Instead of letting our financial struggles and the fear they generated drive us, we resolved to take complete charge of the company's future direction, change it to make a huge impact in the world instead of being just another business, and do what was necessary to achieve this vision. Soon, we began enjoying our work a lot more; we were helping our clients achieve a significant social purpose, and our company started enjoying greater financial success, soon becoming a leader in our market. I learned that making deliberate, proactive choices carries a huge amount of power, opening up many more possibilities for change than would otherwise be available.

Choose to see fear as a gift. During my most terrifying moments, I learned to turn my thoughts to my Creator, the source from which all life comes, in order to seek courage from this light. For example, I was previously extremely fearful of singing in public. My fear was driven by my belief that I had a terrible singing voice, could not hold a tune, and that I would make mistakes when singing publicly. But in my heart, I really wanted to sing. So I took coaching lessons, asked my coach how she thought I was doing, and gathered the courage to sing in front of a very small audience after practicing countless times. It went well, and slowly I gained confidence. Each time I sang, I would tell myself that the same force that creates the majesty of nature and the human body was in me, around me, and beside me. With such light enveloping me, how could I not sing brilliantly? And sing well I did, time and time again, to my surprise and to the surprise of those around me. Bit by bit, I have learned that things will turn out the way they are meant to, that there is a grand universal plan for me, and that my life has deep purpose. I have reestablished my deep spiritual connectedness with the universe, something that I was privileged to enjoy in my teens, thanks to the lessons, teachings, and example of my wonderful parents.

Choose to recognize your fears to understand your belief system. Knowing and understanding my fears made me start thinking about my belief system. For example, when I analyzed my thoughts about money, I realized that I had deep-rooted negative beliefs about money: as the source of all evil, at cross-purposes to faith, a zero-sum game (if I had more, someone had to have less), etc. So at that point, it was no wonder that I was not achieving the financial success that I knew myself capable of. After all, with such negative affirmations, there was no way the universe was going to be showering me with money any time soon! Once I understood my beliefs, I could see the behavior these negative beliefs about money generated and why this behavior was yielding poor results. As I cleared up those negative beliefs, the world's abundance began appearing at my doorstep.

So again, think of as many fears as you can, and for the moment, simply accept these fears: they are an incredible gift that you can use to your advantage, as you will soon find out.

Step 3: Leverage your fears

You now have a much better sense of the fears that have been driving you and how they might be showing up in your life. You know that instead of fighting these fears, you can embrace them by choosing to deal with them proactively. You can perceive fear as a gift that allows you to re-examine your spirituality and choose to see your fears as beacons to understanding your belief system. We *all* have the ability to reframe our fears.

How can you start leveraging your fears in order to realize the plans you made in the previous chapters and have your grand life purpose come true, so that you may light up the world?

Let's examine the beliefs that these fears generate, your behaviors that result from these beliefs, and the results those behaviors yield. This can be a challenging exercise, but one that you will benefit from tremendously. I urge you to take your time and complete the exercise below as fully as possible, even if it means coming back to it several times over the next few days, weeks, or months. I am convinced that your insights will set you free from your fears and will enable you to realize everything you have worked on in previous chapters, as the process did for me.

As you work through this next exercise, you will have started on a wonderful journey that will take your life to a whole new level. Why? Simply because:

1. By identifying your fears, you can understand your beliefs

2. By understanding your beliefs, you can examine your behaviors

3. By becoming highly conscious of your behaviors, you can make changes to produce positive outcomes

4. By producing more positive outcomes, you change your life and that of others

Take the ten predominant fears you just defined and list them below. Then, based on the beliefs and behaviors that you just listed and any others you can think of, complete the exercise below. As you complete each of the ten parts, you will discover that you *do* have control over your fears and that you *can* control them and not let fear dominate your life anymore.

1. **The fear I am embracing is**

    _____

    My **beliefs** related to this fear are:

    _____
    _____
    _____

    My **behaviors** stemming from these beliefs are:

    _____
    _____
    _____

    Since I have complete control over my behaviors, I promise myself I will make the following changes:

    _____
    _____
    _____

2. **The fear I am embracing is**

    _____

    My **beliefs** related to this fear are:

    _____
    _____
    _____

    My **behaviors** stemming from these beliefs are:

    _____
    _____
    _____

    Since I have complete control over my behaviors, I promise myself I will make the following changes:

    _____
    _____
    _____

3. The fear I am embracing is

_____

My **beliefs** related to this fear are:

_____

_____

_____

My **behaviors** stemming from these beliefs are:

_____

_____

_____

Since I have complete control over my behaviors, I promise myself I will make the following changes:

_____

_____

_____

4. The fear I am embracing is

_____

My **beliefs** related to this fear are:

_____

_____

_____

My **behaviors** stemming from these beliefs are:

_____

_____

_____

Since I have complete control over my behaviors, I promise myself I will make the following changes:

_____

_____

_____

5. The fear I am embracing is

_____

My **beliefs** related to this fear are:

_____

_____

_____

My **behaviors** stemming from these beliefs are:

_____

_____

_____

Since I have complete control over my behaviors, I promise myself I will make the following changes:

_____

_____

_____

6. The fear I am embracing is

_____

My **beliefs** related to this fear are:

_____

_____

_____

My **behaviors** stemming from these beliefs are:

_____

_____

_____

Since I have complete control over my behaviors, I promise myself I will make the following changes:

_____

_____

_____

7. The fear I am embracing is

_____

My **beliefs** related to this fear are:

_____

_____

_____

My **behaviors** stemming from these beliefs are:

_____

_____

_____

Since I have complete control over my behaviors, I promise myself I will make the following changes:

_____

_____

_____

8. The fear I am embracing is

_____

My **beliefs** related to this fear are:

_____

_____

_____

My **behaviors** stemming from these beliefs are:

_____

_____

_____

Since I have complete control over my behaviors, I promise myself I will make the following changes:

_____

_____

_____

9. The fear I am embracing is

_____

My **beliefs** related to this fear are:

_____

_____

_____

My **behaviors** stemming from these beliefs are:

_____

_____

_____

Since I have complete control over my behaviors, I promise myself I will make the following changes:

_____

_____

_____

10. The fear I am embracing is

_____

My **beliefs** related to this fear are:

_____

_____

_____

My **behaviors** stemming from these beliefs are:

_____

_____

_____

Since I have complete control over my behaviors, I promise myself I will make the following changes:

_____

_____

_____

This worksheet is contained within the free, downloadable workbook at www.KeepAnyPromise.com/workbook.

When you choose to adopt a much more empowering belief system than you have had in the past, you will find that your behaviors change, that the freedom you gain from embracing and leveraging your fears allows you much greater freedom, and that you start making changes in your life, big and small. As you make these changes, the results you get will change, too. This is a universal truth, so go ahead and try it: changing your thinking about your fears *will* change your life.

Chapter 29:

What Part Do Affirmations Play?

Learn to think in positive affirmations. Affirmations are any statements you make. Too often we think in negative affirmations. Negative affirmations only create more of what you say you don't want.

—*Louise Hay*

In making changes in my life—and goal setting, by its very nature, involves change—I have found it incredibly powerful to start my day with affirmations. And affirmations are a powerful way to overcome fears.

What is an affirmation? It is a positive, short statement that you repeat to yourself to help you work toward a goal or overcome a fear in a positive frame of mind. Below are thirteen affirmations, and space for you to add others. Simply choose ten affirmations that you most relate to, type or write these up, and then daily, when getting dressed, when out for a walk, when driving to work, **recite aloud** your ten affirmations. Soon, you will have memorized them.

1. "All I need is within me now."

2. "Every day, in every way, I'm getting stronger and stronger."

3. "The world's abundance is here to serve me."

4. "I am joy and joy flows through me."

5. "I love my life, and I am so blessed."

6. "Wealth is circulating in my life. I have abundance."

7. "All my needs, desires, and goals are met and I give thanks."

8. "My body moves and it serves me. I am strong. I am capable."

9. "I expect nothing. I cherish silence."

10. "I trust my purpose to guide me to the right decisions."

11. "I feel completely supported in whatever I am doing."

12. "I embrace this moment, and cherish it, for I am free of my past: it is gone, forever."

13. "I can exceed any challenge I set out to conquer."

Add your own favorite affirmations below.

▶▶	
▶▶	
▶▶	
▶▶	
▶▶	
▶▶	
▶▶	
▶▶	
▶▶	

I found that when I started using affirmations, I did not completely believe each one. Some of them, especially involving my health and body, were an enormous stretch for me. Gradually, I started trusting them more and more, and, amazingly, my body started reacting and my health started improving.

So pick ten affirmations from above with which you most identify. Add more affirmations gradually if you wish, and trust that over time, the affirmations, repeated persistently and with emotion, *will* give you the results you desire. I believe there are two reasons why this is so.

First, it's simply the Law of Attraction. If you never ask the universe for what you want, how will you ever attract it? Conversely, when you are clear and persistent about what you see and feel, the universe responds.

Secondly, by strongly inculcating these thoughts into your mind, especially your subconscious mind, your mind starts seeing opportunities. Your mind also refocuses your behaviors on those activities and thoughts that it receives via your clear and precise incantations.

A wonderful resource for affirmations is http://www.affirmware.com.au.

Chapter 30:

What's the Next Step?

Any fact facing us is not as important as our attitude toward it, for that determines our success or failure. The way you think about a fact may defeat you before you ever do anything about it. You are overcome by the fact because you think you are.

—*Norman Vincent Peale*

Y ou've been on quite a journey of discovery through this book, as you've read the inspirational stories and worked through the many worksheets. After completing Part 1 of the book, I hope that you have mastered the twelve steps to thinking about any goal and that this is now second nature. Achieving goals is key to keeping your promises! I hope that you have been able to take the concepts in Part 2 and integrate them into your life, so that there is a rhythmic pattern of movement and progress on your goals each day, week, month, quarter, and year. And after completing the demanding exercises in Part 3, I hope you have a much clearer vision for your life. Most important, what have you learned about yourself? I hope above all else, you have learned that you, too, can achieve *any* dream, accomplish *any* goal, and keep *any* promise. You, too, can let *your* light shine to illuminate the world.

The key to sustained and ever-increasing progress is to consistently follow a simple system. I have outlined three key initial steps below:

1. If you have not yet completed the worksheets, you owe it to yourself to go back and do so soon. Very soon. Or you may well face a lifetime of continued broken promises. Wouldn't that be awful, especially when the alternative is so much more attractive and so attainable?

2. Schedule key planning phases. Whether you use a paper method or Microsoft Outlook or any other computer-based calendar, set time aside (*now*) in your calendar for thinking about and developing:

    a. An annual plan (five-hour appointment with yourself per year)

    b. A ninety-day plan (two-hour appointment per quarter)

    c. A monthly plan (two-hour appointment per month)

    d. A weekly plan (half-hour appointment per week)

    To put it in perspective, this amounts to about sixty hours spread out over the year, about half of one percent of your time per year. Surely your life is worth this much planning and reflection time? **Book these appointments into your calendar now. Think of these as your most critical appointments of the year, ones that you commit to keeping no matter what your circumstances.**

3. Reserve ten minutes each day to maintain your Daily Journal; ask yourself the seven magical questions in Chapter 19.

If you find you need additional assistance with thinking through some of these life-changing materials and concepts and in sustaining changes in your life, here are some options you should strongly consider.

1. **Participate in a two-day Life Makeover seminar or eight-week online seminar with me.** I guarantee that you will come away with an incredible blueprint for your life that will help you soar, or we will refund your full fee. Just use the code at the end of the book at www. KeepAnyPromise.com/lifemakeover to obtain a deep discount.

2. **Become an affiliate** and help us get the word out to thousands of people so that their lives may be enriched. To do so, simply join our generous affiliate program at www.KeepAnyPromise.com/affiliates. I know that everyone you refer who orders a book, an e-book, or the audiobook, or who participates in the Life Makeover will thank you for your help. In addition, you could earn thousands of dollars in affiliate revenue each year.

   I pledge that 25 percent of the profits from book sales, e-book sales, audiobook sales, seminars and webinars, and teleseminars at www.KeepAnyPromise.com will be donated to registered charities around the world. So join me in helping make a difference in the lives of many people and causes.

I wish you a lifetime of tranquility, success, good health, and happiness.

In gratitude,

Karim H. Ismail

Resources

Over the last few years, I have read many books, attended many seminars, and listened to many audio books by some wonderful authors and thought leaders. They are listed below. To link easily to these resources in order to get additional information, please go to www.KeepAnyPromise.com/resources.

Web site: http://www.affirmware.com.au

Book: Allen, James. *The Wisdom of James Allen.* San Diego: Laurel Creek Press, 1997.

Book: Barker, Gail, and Gail Nielsen. *The Control Freak's Guide to Living Lightly.* Strathroy, ON: Power of Two Publishing, 2006.

Book: Cameron, Julia. *Answered Prayers.* New York: Jeremy P. Tarcher/Putnam, 2004.

Book: Cameron, Julia. *Blessings: Prayers and Declarations for a Heartful Life.* New York: Jeremy P. Tarcher/Putnam, 1998.

Book: Cameron, Julia. *God is No Laughing Matter: Observations and Objections on the Spiritual Path.* New York: Jeremy P. Tarcher/Putnam, 2000.

Book: Cameron, Julia. *Heart Steps: Prayers and Declarations for a Creative Life.* New York: Jeremy P. Tarcher/Putnam, 1997.

Book: Cameron, Julia. *Transitions: Prayers and Declarations for a Changing Life.* New York: Jeremy P. Tarcher/Putnam, 1999.

Book: Cameron, Julia. *The Right to Write.* New York: Jeremy P. Tarcher/Putnam, 1998.

Book: Chopra, Deepak. *The Book of Secrets: Unlocking the Hidden Dimensions of Your Life*. New York: Harmony Books, 2004.

Book: Chopra, Deepak. *Creating Affluence—Wealth Consciousness in the Field of All Possibilities*. San Rafael, CA: New World Library, 1993.

Book: Chopra, Deepak. *The Seven Spiritual Laws Of Success: A Practical Guide to the Fulfillment of Your Dreams*. San Rafael, CA: New World Library/Amber-Allen Publishing, 1994.

Book: DeVrye, Catherine. *Hot Lemon and Honey: Reflections for Success in Times of Stress and Change*. Toronto: Warwick Publishing, Inc., 2003.

Book: Diamond, Harvey, and Marilyn Diamond. *Fit for Life*. New York: Warner Books, 1985.

Book: Dyer, Wayne W. *10 Secrets For Success And Inner Peace*. Carlsbad, CA: Hay House, 2002.

Book: Dyer, Wayne W. *Being in Balance: 9 Principles for Creating Habits to Match Your Desires*. Carlsbad, CA: Hay House, 2006.

Book: Dyer, Wayne W. *Change your Thoughts—Change your Life: Living the Wisdom of the Tao*. Carlsbad, CA: Hay House, 2007.

Book: Dyer, Wayne W. *Everyday Wisdom for Success*. Carlsbad, CA: Hay House, 2006.

Book: Dyer, Wayne W. *Inspiration: Your Ultimate Calling*. Carlsbad, CA: Hay House, 2006.

Book: Dyer, Wayne W. *Manifest your Destiny: The Nine Spiritual Principles for Getting Everything You Want*. New York: Harper Paperbacks, 1999.

Book: Dyer, Wayne W. *Real Magic: Creating Miracles in Everyday Life*. New York: HarperCollins Publishers, 1992.

CD set: Dyer, Wayne W. *The Secrets of the Power of Intention: Learning to Co-create Your World Your Way*. Carlsbad, CA: Hay House, 2007.

Book: Dyer, Wayne W. *You'll See It When You Believe It: The Way to Your Personal Transformation.* New York: HarperCollins Publishers, 1989.

Book: Guinness, Os. *The Call: Finding and Fulfilling the Central Purpose of Your Life.* Nashville: W Publishing Group (Thomas Nelson), 2003.

Book: His Holiness the Dalai Lama and Victor Chan. *The Wisdom of Forgiveness.* New York: Riverhead Books, 2004.

Book: Jeffers, Susan. *Feel the Fear and Do It Anyway.* New York: Ballantine Books, 1988.

Book: Jeffers, Susan. *Feel the Fear ... and Beyond: Mastering the Techniques for Doing It Anyway.* New York: Ballantine Books, 1998.

Speech: King, Martin Luther. "I Have A Dream." Washington, DC, August 28, 1963.

Book: Kripalani, Krishna, ed. *All Men Are Brothers: Life and Thoughts of Mahatma Gandhi As Told in His Own Words.* Ahmedabad: Navajivan Publishing House, 1960.

Speech: Mandela, Nelson. "I Am Prepared To Die," statement from the dock at the opening of the defense case in the Rivonia trial. Pretoria Supreme Court, 20 April 1964.

E-book: Mayo, Stacey. *Is Your Ladder Leaning Against the Wrong Wall?* Mableton, GA: Centre for Balanced Living, 2005.

Book: Millman, Dan. *Way of the Peaceful Warrior: A Book That Changes Lives.* Tiburon, CA: HJ Kramer, 2006.

Book: Nomura, Catherine and Babs Smith, eds. *The Quotable Dan Sullivan.* Toronto: The Strategic Coach, Inc., 2004.

Book: Nomura, Catherine, Julia Waller, and Shannon Waller. *Unique Ability®: Creating The Life You Want.* Toronto: The Strategic Coach, 1995-2007.

Seminar: Robbins, Tony. *Date with Destiny.* Bahamas, 2003.

CD set: Robbins, Tony. *Get the Edge: A 7-Day Program to Transform Your Emotions, Relationships, Health, Finances ... and Your Life.* Robbins Research International, Inc., 1999.

Seminar: Robbins, Tony. *Life Mastery.* Palm Springs, 2005

Multimedia Program: Robbins, Tony. *The Time of Your Life: More Time for What Really Matters to You.* Robbins Research International, Inc., 1998.

Multimedia Program: Robbins, Tony and Cloé Madanes. *Ultimate Relationship Program.* Robbins-Madanes Center for Strategic Intervention, 2005.

Seminar: Robbins, Tony. *Unleash the Power Within.* Denver, 2003

Film Series: Robbins-Madanes Center for Strategic Intervention. *Inner Strength Series.* 2004

Book: Schwartz, David. *The Magic of Thinking Big.* New York: Fireside (Simon & Schuster, Inc.), 1987.

Book: Sharma, Robin. *Discover Your Destiny With The Monk Who Sold His Ferrari.* Toronto: HarperCollins Publishers Ltd., 2004.

Book: Sharma, Robin. *Family Wisdom From The Monk Who Sold His Ferrari.* Toronto: HarperCollins Publishers Ltd., 2001.

Book: Sharma, Robin. *Leadership Wisdom From The Monk Who Sold His Ferrari.* Toronto: HarperCollins Publishers Ltd., 1998.

Book: Sharma, Robin. *The Monk Who Sold His Ferrari.* New York: HarperCollins Publishers, 1999.

Book: Sharma, Robin. *The Saint, The Surfer & The CEO.* Carlsbad, CA: Hay House, 2002.

Book: Sharma, Robin. *Who Will Cry When You Die?* Carlsbad, CA: Hay House, 2002.

Multimedia Program: Sullivan, Dan. *Always Increase Your Confidence* series. Toronto: The Strategic Coach, Inc. 2002-2006.

Multimedia Program: Sullivan, Dan. *The 21-Day Positive Focus.* Toronto: The Strategic Coach, Inc., 1999-2008.

Multimedia Program: Sullivan, Dan. *The D.O.S. Conversation.* Toronto: The Strategic Coach, Inc., 1994-2007.

Multimedia Program: Sullivan, Dan. *Goal Cultivator* series. Toronto: The Strategic Coach, Inc., 2002-2005.

Multimedia Program: Sullivan, Dan. *The Gratitude Principle.* Toronto: The Strategic Coach, Inc., 1999-2006.

Book: Sullivan, Dan. *The Great Crossover.* With Babs Smith and Michel Néray. Toronto: The Strategic Coach, Inc., 1994-2000.

Audio CD and Book: Sullivan, Dan. *How The Best Get Better.* Toronto: The Strategic Coach, Inc., 1996-2007.

Audio CD and Book: Sullivan, Dan. *How The Best Get Better 2.* Toronto: The Strategic Coach, Inc., 2007.

Book: Sullivan, Dan and Catherine Nomura. *The Laws of Lifetime Growth.* Toronto: Berrett-Koehler Publishers, 2006.

Audio CD and mini-book: Sullivan, Dan. *Learning How To Avoid The Gap.* Toronto: The Strategic Coach, Inc., 1999-2007.

Multimedia Program: Sullivan, Dan. *The Time Breakthrough.* Toronto: The Strategic Coach, Inc., 1999-2006.

Book: Tolle, Eckhart. *Practicing the Power of Now: Essential Teachings, Meditations, and Exercises from The Power of Now.* Novato, CA: New World Library, 1999.

Book: Tolle, Eckhart. *Stillness Speaks.* Vancouver: Namaste Publishing, 2003.

Book: Williamson, Marianne. *A Return To Love: Reflections on the Principles of "A Course in Miracles"* New York: HarperCollins Publishers, Inc., 1996.

This certificate entitles you,
your friends and family to

50% off

the **Life Makeover** seminars at
www.KeepAnyPromise.com.

Please use this code,
7861234A

when purchasing these items.

This certificate entitles you to a

FREE
Life Blueprint Workbook
worth $149

at www.KeepAnyPromise.com.

Please use this code,

7869999A

when checking out this item.

You can become an affiliate at www.KeepAnyPromise.com
and encourage your friends and family to get their own
copy of the book, ebook, or audiobook, so that they
can download their own version of the workbook.

Printed in Great Britain
by Amazon